THE BEST OF
SCIENCE
FICTION
TV

**The Critics' Choice
from Captain Video
to Star Trek,
from The Jetsons
to Robotech**

By JOHN JAVNA

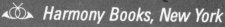

Harmony Books, New York

This book is dedicated to the Future.
Hi there, Gideon.
Hi there, Sam.

Published by Harmony Books, a division of Crown Publishers, Inc., 225 Park Avenue South, New York, NY 10003 and represented in Canada by the Canadian MANDA Group.

HARMONY and colophon are trademarks of Crown Publishers, Inc.

Manufactured in the United States of America

Design by Andrea Sohn

Library of Congress Cataloging-in-Publication Data
Javna, John
    The best of science fiction TV.
    Bibliography: p.
    1. Science fiction television programs. I. Title.
PN 1992.8.S35J38 1987 791.45'09'09356 87-21120

ISBN 0-517-56650-8
10 9 8 7 6 5 4 3 2 1
First Edition

ACKNOWLEDGMENTS

First, I'd like to express my gratitude to the more than one hundred experts who took the time to speak with or write to me about science fiction TV. Many of you went way out of your way to help, even though we'd never met. You're all listed in the introduction, so I won't name each of you here. But I did want to single out **Peter Pautz**, secretary of the Science Fiction Writers of America, and **Jeff Borden**, secretary of the Television Critics Association. It literally would have been impossible to write this book without your assistance, and I appreciate it very much.

MANY THANKS TO

Melissa Schwarz, my editor at Harmony, a source of strength, a pleasure to work with, and one of the nicest people I've met in the book world.

Andrea Sohn, who designed the book, stuck with the project, and managed to stay sane when I wasn't anywhere close. For me, the luckiest part of the project.

Ron McCutchan, Harmony's Art Director, who helped us pull it all together.

The editors of *Starlog*, particularly **David McDonnell** and **Carr D'Angelo**.

John Peel, a virtual TV encyclopedia who rushed me photos, helped with the writing, dictated details over the phone, and even checked the manuscript for accuracy.

Joel Eisner, who helped tremendously with the Japanimation and "Ultraman" stuff, and supplied photos.

Gary H. Grossman, who rushed me his Golden Age photos and kindly permitted the use of quotes from *Saturday Morning T.V.*

Fred Patten, who just happened to be home when I called, and wound up supplying a wealth of information about Japanese animation.

Jay Nitschke and **Doug Burnet** at Co-op Type, who took over when I took off and provided months of advice on desktop publishing.

Mike Dougan, who provided introductions and moral support that helped me get started.

AND

• **Rob Wilson, Tom Hermstad,** and **Bob Fink** at Byting Your Time, who got the book typeset when we needed it yesterday.
• **Sandy Ferguson** at "Legwork,"my reliable researcher.
• **Cherry Steffey** of Scorpio.
• **Sue Moore**.
• **Cheryl Gerber** of *Channels* magazine.
• **Mathey Simon** at Orion.
• **Ivey Orta** and **Anna Gustafson** at Columbia Pictures.
• **Kathy Leech** at MCA.
• **Ed Gilbert** at ITC.
• **Quinn Martin.**
• **Linda Rosenbaum** and **Sarah Baisley** at Hanna-Barbera.
• **Kate Kessler** at Harmony Gold.
• **Grace Darby** at *The New Yorker*.
• **Ray Craft** at Lionheart, for trying to get through to England.
• **Sharon.**

P.S.: I got a letter from my friend, **Kevin McGarvey**, the other day. He had a good-natured complaint: After all the time he spent listening to my rock 'n' roll stories while I was writing *Behind the Hits* in Mexico, I forgot to list him in the acknowledgments of the book. Well, sorry Kevin. Here's a belated thank-you.

3

CONTENTS

THE WORST TEN

THE CLASSICS

INTRODUCTION

THE TOP FIFTEEN

CONTENTS

CULT FAVORITES

"Look, I write prose fiction. I've never done anything for Hollywood except accept their money for projects that didn't come off, and I don't have a lot of respect for most of their product. So asking me to talk about this stuff is like asking me what my favorite kind of cockroach is."

—*Science fiction writer Robert Silverberg, responding to questions about his favorite sf TV shows.*

SCIENCE FICTION TV

After interviewing close to one hundred thoughtful and articulate critics about science fiction TV, I've come to this conclusion: Commercial television and true science fiction are fundamentally incompatible. Television is the protector and perpetuator of the status quo; its primary purpose is to pacify, to lull its audience into a vaguely secure, pliable state and make them receptive to advertisers' messages. Science fiction, on the other hand, exists solely to shake its audience into aware-

ness—to force people to question and think, to gaze at their own lives with a new—often frightening—perspective. Commercial television can soothe or excite a viewer; good science fiction throttles him.

Despite this contradiction, TV keeps experimenting with the genre. It's surprising how often, in fact. Since 1950, more than one hundred science fiction programs have been launched through the airwaves. Can't name them? Even die-hard fans would be hard pressed to dredge up memories of "Space G-Men" or "Prince Dinosaur." And it's a safe bet that no one but die-hard fans would *want* to watch them.

As a matter of fact, judging by the Nielsens, die-hard fans may be the only people watching the better-known shows, too. In the last thirty-five years, only one series billed as a science fiction show has ever ranked in the Top 20 of a year.

It wasn't "Star Trek" (whose best showing was #52). Or "The Twilight Zone." Or "The Outer Limits." It was Jack Webb's "Project UFO," a show described by critics as "*National Enquirer* television" and "Just the aliens, ma'am." It tied for #19 in the 1977-78 season.

THE POLL

Of course, quality and ratings have nothing to do with each other; so this book proffers a different yardstick for measuring science fiction TV's success—the opinions of critics.

Between February and March 1987, in a poll conducted exclusively for *The Best of Science Fiction TV*, over one hundred experts were asked to name the

Top 15 and Worst 10 science fiction series ever presented on television.

The survey was created in stages.

First, the editors of *Starlog* magazine, the premier sf media publication in America, nominated twenty-five shows for "best" and twenty for "worst" sf series. The editors, David McDonnell, Carr D'Angelo, Eddie Berganza, and Daniel Dickholtz, understood that this was to be a poll specifically about science fiction—not fantasy or horror—and selected accordingly.

Stage two: Their list was reviewed by a panel of three TV critics.

And finally, a questionnaire was assembled and sent to participants. It listed the nominees, but also encouraged write-ins.

Originally the survey was designed to query only TV critics. However, on reflection, that seemed inappropriate. TV critics know what makes a good TV show, but they don't necessarily understand what makes good science fiction. A poll is only as accurate as its sampling, so the survey was expanded to include

The Jetsons, © 1987 Hanna-Barbera Productions Inc.

a variety of additional viewpoints: science fiction writers (whose work defines the genre), science fiction critics, TV historians, and members of a number of fan organizations.

We sought diversity within each group—all ages, all geographical areas. Among sf writers, varied style and experience counted. The fan organizations were selected to represent different areas of the country; however, we included only general science fiction groups, because it seemed unlikely that a "Dr. Who" or "Star Trek" group would be objective.

Most of the science fiction writers were reached through their national organization, The Science Fiction Writers of America, with the encouragement and assistance of Peter Pautz, their executive secretary. Most TV critics were reached with the help of Jeff Borden, Secretary of the Television Critics' Association.

And by the way—Mr. Silverberg, who is a true gentleman, did indeed add his list of favorite "cockroaches" to this effort.

SCORING

After experts submitted lists of their Top 15 and Worst 10 sf shows (or less, if they felt there weren't enough worthy programs), the programs they named were assigned points.

The scoring system worked like this:

In the Top 15 voting, each first place show received 20 points; each second place received 17; each third place received 14; fourth got 12, fifth, 11; sixth, 10; seventh, 9; eighth, 8; ninth, 7; tenth, 6; eleventh, 5;

twelfth, 4; thirteenth, 3; fourteenth, 2; fifteenth, 1.

In the Worst 10 voting, each show selected as worst received 15 points; runner-up received 12; third place received 9; fourth, 7; fifth, 6; sixth, 5; seventh, 4; eighth, 3; ninth, 2; tenth, 1.

THE RESULTS

THE BEST

1. "Star Trek"
2. "The Twilight Zone" (the 1959-65 version)
3. "The Outer Limits"
4. "The Hitchhiker's Guide to the Galaxy"
5. "Dr. Who"
6. "Amazing Stories"
7. "Mork and Mindy"
8. "The Wild, Wild West"
9. "V" (the miniseries)
10. "The Prisoner"
11. "The Invaders"
12. "Quark"
13. "The Jetsons"
14. "Captain Video"
15. "The Adventures of Superman"
16. "Space Patrol"

17. "Tom Corbett, Space Cadet"
18. "The Twilight Zone" (1980s version)
19. "Lost in Space"
20. "Way Out"
21. "The Avengers"
22. "Battlestar Galactica"
23. "Science Fiction Theater"
24. "My Favorite Martian"
25. "Blake's 7"

Other programs named on at least three ballots: "ALF," "Automan," "Batman," "Buck Rogers in the 25th Century," "Captain Nice," "The Champions," "Flash Gordon," "The Greatest American Hero," "The Incredible Hulk," "Jonny Quest," "Kolchak, the Night Stalker," "Land of the Lost," "The Man from UNCLE.," "Men Into Space," "Night Gallery," "One Step Beyond," "Otherworld," "The Phoenix," "The Questor Tapes," "Space: 1999," "Tales from the Darkside," "Tales of Tomorrow," "The Time Tunnel," "Voyage to the Bottom of the Sea," "Voyagers."

INTRODUCTION

THE WORST

1. "Space: 1999"
2. "Buck Rogers in the 25th Century"
3. "Galactica 1980"
4. "The Powers of Matthew Star"
5. "Battlestar Galactica"
6. "Lost in Space"
7. "The Man from Atlantis"
8. "The Starlost"
9. "Voyage to the Bottom of the Sea"
10. "It's About Time"
11. "Logan's Run"
12. "Project UFO"
13. "Otherworld"
14. "The Time Tunnel"
15. "Far Out Space Nuts"
16. "The Lost Saucer"
17. "Land of the Giants"
18. "V" (the series)
19. "Fantastic Journey"
20. "Automan"

Other programs named on at least three ballots: "Amazing Stories," "The Bionic Woman," "Blake's 7," "Dr. Who," "The Invisible Man" (1975 version), "The Jetsons," "Misfits of Science," "My Favorite Martian," "The New Wonder Woman," "The Phoenix," "The Planet of the Apes," "The Six-Million Dollar Man," "Starman," "V" (the miniseries).

The most unusual choice for best was "The Andy Griffith Show." The most unusual choice for worst was "CBS Morning News with Phyllis George."

Here is a complete list of individuals and organizations who voted in the poll; my sincere thanks to all of the participants:

TV CRITICS

- **Greg Bailey**, TV critic, *Nashville Banner*
- **Robert Bianco**, TV critic, *Pittsburgh Press*
- **David Bianculli,** TV critic, *New York Post*
- **Jeff Borden**, TV critic, *Charlotte Observer*
- **Jill Brooke**, TV and radio reporter, *New York Post*
- **John Burlingame**, *TV Data*
- **John Carman**, TV critic, *San Francisco Chronicle*
- **Bob Curtwright**, TV columnist/movie critic, *Wichita Eagle-Beacon*
- **David Cuthbert**, TV editor, *New Orleans Times-Picayune*
- **Mark Dawidziak**, TV critic, *Akron Beacon Journal*
- **Michael Dougan**, TV critic, *San Francisco Examiner*
- **Rick Du Brow**, TV editor, *Los Angeles Herald Examiner*
- **Duane Dudek**, TV/Film Editor, *Milwaukee Sentinel*
- **Michael Duffy**, TV critic, *Detroit Free Press*
- **Peter Farrell**, TV columnist, *Oregonian*
- **Bob Foster**, TV critic, *San Mateo Times*
- **Barry Garron**, TV/Radio critic, *Kansas City Star*
- **Marc Gunther**, TV critic, *Detroit News*
- **R. D. Heldenfels**, TV columnist, *Schenectady Gazette*
- **Michael Hill**, TV critic, *Baltimore Evening Sun*
- **Ken Hoffman**, TV critic, *Houston Post*
- **Barbara Holsopple**, TV critic, *Phoenix Gazette*
- **Noel Holston**, TV critic, *Minneapolis Star and Tribune*
- **Tom Jicha**, TV editor, *Miami News*
- **David Jones**, TV critic, *Columbus Dispatch*
- **Marvin Kitman**, TV critic, *Newsday*
- **Robert P. Laurence**, TV writer, *San Diego Union*
- **Eric Mink**, TV critic, *St. Louis Post Dispatch*
- **Susan Paynter**, TV critic, *Seattle Post-Intelligencer*
- **Joel Pisetzner**, TV critic, *Bergen Record*
- **Daniel Ruth**, TV critic, *Chicago Sun-Times*
- **Dusty Saunders**, TV critic, *Rocky Mountain News*
- **Pat Sellers**, New York correspondent, *Toronto Star, Starweek, TV Magazine*
- **Tom Shales**, TV critic *Washington Post*
- **R.K. Shull**, TV critic, *Indianapolis News*
- **Ed Siegel**, TV critic, *Boston Globe*
- **Debbi Snook**, TV critic, *Cleveland Plain Dealer*
- **Steve Sonsky**, TV critic, *Miami Herald*
- **Joseph Walker**, TV critic, *Salt Lake City Deseret News*
- **Bob Wisehart**, TV columnist, *Sacramento Bee*

INTRODUCTION

MEMBERS OF THE SCIENCE FICTION WRITERS OF AMERICA

•**Pat Cadigan**, author of *Mindplayers* (Bantam) and numerous short stories appearing in *Omni, Isaac Asimov's Fantasy and Science Fiction, Twilight Zone, Shadows,* and *Mirrorshades*

•**Jeffrey A. Carver**, author of six sf novels, including *The Infinity Link*

•**Michael Cassutt**, former CBS network programming executive; author of fiction and nonfiction; staff writer for "Twilight Zone"; story editor for "Max Headroom"

•**Michael Berlyn**, author of three novels (*The Integrated Man, Crystal Phoenix, After the Change*) and six works of interactive fiction (*Suspended, Cyborg, Oo-Topos, Infidel, Cutthroats, Tass Times in Tonetown, Rager*)

•**C.J. Cherryh**, science fiction writer (*The Faded Sun, Hunter of Worlds,* etc.)

•**Jack Dann**, author or editor of twenty-one books, including the novels *Junction, Starhiker, The Man Who Melted,* and the mainstream novel *Counting Coup*

•**George Alec Effinger**, science fiction author (*The Bird of Time, When Gravity Fails,* etc.)

•**David Gerrold**, screenwriter and science fiction novelist

•**Robert Jordan**, author (*Conan the Magnificent,* etc.) and editor

•**Lee Killough**, secretary, Science Fiction Writers of America; Hugo nominee, short story category

•**Nancy Kress**, author of four novels and one short story collection, which includes "Out of All Them Bright Stars," Nebula-winning story for 1986

•**Dean R. Lambe, Ph.D.**, science fiction writer and reviewer

•**Fritz Leiber**, science fiction author (*The Swords of Lankhmar, The Green Millennium,* etc.)

•**Pat Murphy**, author of *The Falling Woman* and *The Shadow Hunter*

•**Warren Norwood**, author of *The Windhover Tapes* series, *The Double-Spiral War* series, *Shudderchild, True Jaguar,* twice nominated for the John W. Campbell Award

•**Peter D. Pautz**, author; executive secretary of SFWA; president, World Fantasy Award

•**Elizabeth Ann Scarborough**, author of *Song of Sorcery, Unicorn Greed, Bronwyn's Bane, Harem of Amah Akbar, Christening Quest, Drastic Dragon of Drako Texas, Them Goldcamp Vampires*

•**Susan Shwartz**, writer, edi-

tor, and critic. Author of *Byzantium's Crown, Silk Roads and Shadows, Heritage of Flight*

•**Robert Silverberg**, science fiction writer (*The Majipoor Trilogy, Tom O'Bedlam,* etc.)

•**Sharon Webb**, author of *Earthchild, Earth Song, Ram Song, The Adventures of Terra Tarkington*

•**F. Paul Wilson**, author of six sf and fantasy novels (*The Tomb, The Touch,* etc.) and numerous short stories

•**Gene Wolfe**, author of *Free Live Free, The Shadow of the Torturer, Soldier of the Mist*

•**Jane Yolen**, author of almost one hundred published books and president of the SFWA

SCIENCE FICTION FAN GROUPS

•**Mark A. Altman**, editor/publisher, *Galactic Journal* magazine

•**D. Douglas Fratz**, editor, *THRUST—Science Fiction and Fantasy Review*

•**David Houston**, science fiction writer, original editor of *Starlog* magazine, journalist

•**David McDonnell**, editor, *Starlog* magazine

•**Douglas Menville**, author of *A Historical and Critical Survey of the Science-Fiction Film, Things to Come: An Illustrated History of the SF Film,* and *Futurevisions: The New Golden Age of the SF Film "*

•**Craig Miller**, motion picture publicist and marketing consultant: *Star Wars, Empire Strikes Back, Altered States, Dark Crystal, Return to Oz, Splash,* others; writer, TV cartoons

•**Ed Naha**, author of *The*

Science Fictionary, The Making of Dune, The Films of Roger Coman, Horrors: From Screen to Scream
•**Andy Porter**, editor, *Science Fiction Chronicle, Starship*; former asst. ed., *Magazine of Fantasy and SF*
•**John R. Racano**, editor of *Warp 4 (The Magazine of Science Fiction, Fantasy, and Horror)*
•**Harold Schechter**, professor of English, Queens College the City University, N.Y. Author of *Film Tricks: Special Effects in the Movies*
•**David J. Schow**, author of *The Outer Limits: The Official Companion*; novelizationist; short story writer and editor of *Silver Scream*, an anthology of horror stories about the cinema
•**John Stanley**, editor/publisher, *Creatures at Large*
•**Bill Warren**, author of *Keep Watching the Skies (SF films of the 1950s)*, assistant on *Walt Lee's Reference Guide to Fantastic Film*
•**Scott Zicree**, author of *The Twilight Zone Companion*; TV writer

GENERAL TV

•**Diane L. Albert**, editor, *The TV Collector* magazine
•**Harry Castleman**, coauthor of *Watching TV* and *The TV Schedule Book*
•**Lawrence Closs**, editor, *Applause* magazine, WHYY TV 12 and 91 FM, Philadelphia
•**Joel Eisner**, author of *The Batman Bat-Book, Sitcoms in Syndication*
•**Jeffrey B. Fuerst**, broadcast historian, associate curator, Museum of Broadcasting
•**Gary Gerani**, author of *Fantastic Television*

•**Gary H. Grossman**, author of *Superman: From Serial to Cereal* and *Saturday Morning T.V.*; producer of "Entertainment This Week"
•**John Javna**, author of *Cult TV, The TV Theme Song Sing-Along Songbooks (Volumes I and II)*, coauthor of *60s!*, and more
•**Gordon Javna**, author of *Tough TV: The Television Guide to Your Mind, Calling All Monomaniacs*, co-author of *60s!*
•**Donna McCrohan**, TV historian, author of *The Honeymooners' Companion*, coauthor of *The Honeymooners' Last Episodes*, author of *The Second City: A Backstage History of Comedy's Hottest Troupe*
•**Alex McNeil**, author of *Total Television, A Comprehensive Guide to Programming from 1948 to the Present*
•**Jack Mingo**, author of *The Official Couch Potato Handbook* and *The Couch Potato Guide to Life*
•**Danny Peary**, author of *Omni's Screen Flights/Screen Fantasies: The Future According to Science Fiction Cinema, Guide for the Film Fanatic, Cult Movies 1, 2, & 3*
•**John Peel**, British author of more than eighty volumes of science fiction criticism; contributing editor to *TV Gold*
•**Walter J. Podrazik**, coauthor of seven books, including *Watching TV: Four Decades of American Television*, and *The TV Schedule Book* (a season-by-season schedule guide to the entire broadcast day)
•**Richard K. Tharp**, publisher, *RERUNS, The Magazine of Television History*
•**Michael Uslan**, motion picture/television producer and writer
•**"Weird Al" Yankovic**, musical satirist

SCIENCE FICTION FAN GROUPS

(Represented either by officers or entire membership)
•**Baton Rouge Science Fiction League, Inc.,** Baton Rouge, LA
•**The Birmingham SF Club,** Birmingham, AL
•**The Denver Area Science Fiction Association,** Denver, CO
•**F.O.S.F.A. (Falls of the Ohio Science Fiction and Fantasy Assoc.)**
•**The Galaxy Club,** Buffalo, NY
•**LEXFA (The Lexington Fantasy Association),** Lexington, KY
•**The Long Island Science Fiction Society,** Long Island, NY
•**The Memphis Science Fiction Association,** Memphis, TN
•**National Fantasy Fan Federation,** Los Angeles, CA
•**The New Jersey Science Fiction Society,** Paramus, NJ
•**Niatrek Information Service,** Niagra Falls, NY
•**Northern California Science Fantasy Association,** Menlo Park, CA
•**The Phoenix Society,** Atlanta, GA
•**The Plutonian Society,** Brighton, MI
•**Quark: The Association of Science Fiction and Fantasy,** Provo, UT
•**Science Fiction and Fantasy Guild. FPCI,** Alhambra, CA
•**The Stone Hill SF Association,** Riverview, FL
•**The Virginia Tech Science Fiction and Fantasy Club,** Blacksburg, VA

The Critics' Choice:
The 15 Best Science Fiction TV Shows of all Time

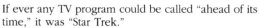

STAR TREK

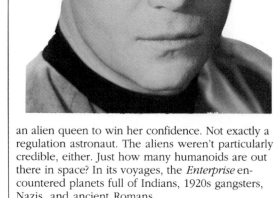

If ever any TV program could be called "ahead of its time," it was "Star Trek."

Today Gene Roddenberry's creation is the force behind books, records, films, and dozens of licensed products; it has grossed hundreds of millions of dollars in syndication; it has earned praise from both fanatical followers and contemporary critics, who named it the best science fiction show of all time in this poll.

But in its original run, "Star Trek" was a flop; in three years—from 1966 to 1969—it never managed to place higher than #52 in the ratings. Critics razzed it as a juvenile space opera with stock spacemen, dime-store aliens, and cheap camera tricks: " 'Star Trek'... won't work," wrote *Variety* magazine. "It's an incredible and dreary mess of confusion and complexities ... [that's] better suited to the Saturday morning kidvid bloc than prime time." Even Gene Roddenberry's father found it embarrassing. "The night 'Star Trek' premiered on television," Roddenberry recalls, "my father excused himself, went out, and walked up and down the street apologizing to all the neighbors."

If this sounds hard to believe, consider it from the critics' point of view. In 1966, there was little precedent for adult science fiction programs on television (actually none at all for a program with continuing characters); so viewers were inclined to compare Captain Kirk to Captain Video. And the crew of the *Enterprise*, for all their appeal, were mostly stereotypes. "Scotty" was the electronic whiz in every TV space adventure; "Bones" was "Doc" from "Gunsmoke;" even Kirk was the typical hero of the "Man from UNCLE" era—a character with some emotional depth and a sense of humor who relied on larger-than-life abilities to overcome the show's weekly menace. In a pinch, Kirk could outthink a murderous robot (Nomad), take on a Godzilla clone (the Gorn) in hand-to-hand combat, or romance

an alien queen to win her confidence. Not exactly a regulation astronaut. The aliens weren't particularly credible, either. Just how many humanoids are out there in space? In its voyages, the *Enterprise* encountered planets full of Indians, 1920s gangsters, Nazis, and ancient Romans.

But there were deeper levels to the show. The three main characters—Spock, Kirk, and McCoy—developed a believable friendship. And Spock's internal struggles, his futile attempts to repress the human side of his personality, were explored in fascinating detail by "Star Trek"'s writers. Above all, there was The Message; in the tradition of the best science fiction, Roddenberry used "Star Trek" as a forum for his ideas about contemporary life. "It was an attempt to make statements about Vietnam, against intolerance, and about things ... that I believe in," he explained.

"Star Trek"'s most enduring quality, however, isn't the topical commentary—it's the show's optimism and abiding faith in humanity. At the end of every episode, Kirk reaffirms the nobility of the human spirit. Viewers are left with a feeling that maybe—just maybe—there's hope for us, after all. In the '80s, messages like that are rare. They've become something to cherish.

FLASHBACK

[Kirk is transported below a planet's surface by aliens. There he finds three throbbing brains under a glass dome.]

KIRK: "Primary mental evolution. Incredible!"

ALIEN 1: "That is not true, Captain. Once we had humanoid form, but we evolved beyond it."

ALIEN 2: "Through eons of devoting ourselves exclusively to intellectual pursuits, we became the physically simple, mentally superior creatures you see before you."

KIRK: "A species that enslaves other beings is hardly superior, mentally or otherwise."

ALIEN 3: "We use only inferior beings."

KIRK: "We have found that *all* life forms in the galaxy are capable of superior development. Perhaps you're not as evolved as you believe."

VITAL STATS

POLL RESULTS:
•First, 1475 pts.

PROGRAM INFO:
•Hour show. NBC
•First show: Sept. 2, 1966
•Last show: Sept. 8, 1969
•78 episodes

BACKGROUND: In the twenty-third century, mankind has learned to live in peace and Earth has joined The United Federation of Planets, a galaxy-wide political organization composed of scores of democratic worlds. Although its members are peaceful, the Federation still maintains a military force—Starfleet—whose armada of space vessels is used to run intergalactic errands, explore new worlds, contact previously unknown civilizations, and defend against its enemies: the Klingons, greasy, goateed, sadistic barbarians; and the Romulans, brilliant descendants of Vulcans, who fought a war against the Federation during the twenty-second century. As we join the *Enterprise*, it is on a five-year mission to explore new worlds and "boldly go where no man has gone before."

THE SHIP AND ITS CREW: The most celebrated of Starfleet's vessels is the starship *Enterprise*, a 190,000-ton Constellation-class cruiser powered by matter/antimatter reaction, which travels at warp speeds, faster than light. Its crew of 428 is commanded by 34-year-old **James Tiberius Kirk** (William Shatner). A native of Riverside, Iowa, Kirk is the youngest captain in Starfleet history. He is compassionate but iron-willed, a moral paragon known throughout the galaxy for his courage, decisiveness, honesty, and sex appeal. Females all over the cosmos have their sights set on him, but he's "married" to his ship.

Kirk has two chief advisors:

•**Mr. Spock** (Leonard Nimoy): The First Officer/Science Officer whose first name is unpronounceable by humans. The half-breed son of Ambassador Sarek of Vulcan and ex-teacher Amanda Grayson of Earth, he considers himself a Vulcan and is devoted to logic.

•**Dr. Leonard "Bones" McCoy** (DeForest Kelley): The passionate Georgia-born Medical Officer who claims to be a "simple country doctor." Actually, he's an expert in space psychology.

•Other prominent crew members include: **Mr. Sulu** (George Takei), Chief Navigator; **Lt. Uhura** (Nichelle Nichols), Communications Officer; **Cmdr. Montgomery Scott** (James Doohan), Chief Engineer; **Nurse Christine Chapel** (Majel Barret), McCoy's assistant; **Ensign Pavel Chekov** (Walter Koenig), Assistant Navigator.

Several different models of the Enterprise were used in "Star Trek." The largest, fourteen feet long, is now hanging in the Smithsonian Institution's Air and Space Museum in Washington, DC. The smallest was a three-inch model, seen in every episode "circling" a planet.

"It sounded like Mickey Mouse time, with the ears."

—Leonard Nimoy

BRIDGE WARS

The banter between McCoy and Spock—logic vs. emotion—was voted "Star Trek"'s most entertaining dialogue:

SPOCK: "It would be a fascinating project."

McCOY: "Fascinating? Those people out there are friends of ours ... if they're still alive!"

SPOCK [deadpan]: "I would say the odds against it are approximately four hundred to ..."

McCOY [frantically]: "Don't quote odds and don't give me any more dispassionate logic, Mr. Spock! Just keep looking!"

SPOCK [raising one eyebrow]:"I would welcome a suggestion, Doctor. Even an emotional one."

TV SPORTS

"Kirk-watching" is a favorite pastime among "Star Trek" aficionados. Using William Shatner's physical condition as a guide, you can always tell the time of year an episode of "Star Trek" was filmed. At the beginning of each season he was in great shape; he looked impressive in the tight-fitting uniforms, and loved to take his shirt off. But as the season wore on, there was no time to exercise—so his gut got bigger and bigger.

The personalities and relationships that became the show's trademark weren't all planned out. Spock, for example, was originally going to be a Martian, and was included in the crew simply because Roddenberry "thought it would be nice to have an alien on board the Enterprise." (NBC didn't agree with him—they suggested, after the first pilot, that Spock be axed.) He had little to do in the two pilots, and became a main character only because scriptwriters found him fascinating. McCoy wasn't even in the pilots, and De-Forest Kelly wasn't listed in the credits as a star until the beginning of the second season.

JUST FOR EFFECT

Special effects weren't "Star Trek"'s strong suit; producers had neither the budget nor the technology to dazzle audiences (even "Lost in Space"'s budget was bigger). But they did have ingenuity. Three of their most memorable effects were achieved with a cartoon, aluminum dust, and colored oil:

1. The glittering effect seen as the transporter dissolved and relocated people's atoms was achieved by tossing aluminum dust into an intense beam of light.
2. The throbbing blobs of color that periodically appeared on the *Enterprise*'s view screen—supposedly giant creatures suspended in space—were actually special dyes that had been dumped into a vat of oil and photographed as they swirled through the liquid.
3. The "zap" beams emanating from the phasers were just animation.

CRITICS' COMMENTS

ABOUT THE CHARACTERS:
"The interplay among the three main characters was beautifully figured out so that it approximates the way we make decisions in life. Think about it. You've got Spock, who is all intellect; you've got McCoy, who is all emotion; and then you've got Kirk in the middle, trying to make the best possible decisions based on a combination of [the two]."
—**Gary Gerani,**
Fantastic Television

ON "TREK"'S INFLUENCE:
" 'Star Trek' has achieved something that very few other shows have ever come close to—it has shifted the viewing audience's perception of what is possible. There are things that have happened in the past twenty years specifically because 'Star Trek' said 'Yea' or 'Nay.' The guys

who got the idea for the compact disc, for example, got it partly because of a 'Star Trek' episode in which information was stored in a library on big silver discs."
—**David Gerrold,**
SF/TV Writer

ABOUT SPECIAL EFFECTS:
"Simple, but not tacky."
—**Ed Siegel,**
Boston Globe

"[They] enhanced the plot, revealing that technology had actually enabled the human race to continue. With it, . . . life didn't end—it prospered."
—**Jill Brooke,**
New York Post

"[I love] the cheapo rock-the-boat scenes on the *Enterprise* whenever it's being attacked."
—**Steve Sonsky,**
Miami Herald

ABOUT KIRK:
"Captain Kirk was born noble and stayed noble throughout the entire series. His character was appealing because he was cerebral—so he was always addressing the big issues, like what humans are here for, how humans should interact, how to succeed through nonviolence. That was different; in 'Gunsmoke,' for example, you never saw Matt Dillon agonizing over whether to pull the trigger."
—**David Bianculli,**
New York Post

ABOUT SPOCK:
"Spock and Ilya Kurakin were probably the two most intelligent comedians on television. ... Spock's deadpan delivery reminded me a lot of Buster Keaton, only with higher SAT scores."
—**Ed Naha,**
The Science Fictionary

"Despite its occasional silliness, 'Star Trek' is a vote of confidence in mankind, a statement that we will survive, resolve our conflicts on Earth, and join together to extend human influence. Gene Roddenberry gave viewers credit for having brains, and they have responded by making it the #1 cult show of all time."   —Michael Dougan, *San Francisco Examiner*

THE TWILIGHT ZONE

"The Twilight Zone" was original, consistently experimental, and unfailingly thought-provoking—which made it unique in its era. "When the show debuted in 1959," Marc Scott Zicree noted in *The Twilight Zone Companion*, "it was a flower blooming in a television desert. ... At a time when the rest of television was hammering home the unstated but nonetheless apparent message that the realities and expectations of life were bracketed within very narrow borders, 'The Twilight Zone' presented a universe of possibilities and options."

Critics appreciated this. "It is a pleasure to report," said *TV Guide* in 1959, "that 'The Twilight Zone,' a Rod Serling enterprise filmed in Hollywood and broadcast on Friday nights by CBS, is the most refreshing new anthology series in some time. It has imagination, highly competent production, and excellent acting. ... But the real star of the series is ... Serling himself. It is the Serling touch that brings 'The Twilight Zone' out of the everyday—and into the beyond."

Serling was unquestionably a television genius, and "The Twilight Zone"'s lasting appeal is a tribute to his vision. The show was *not* exclusively a science fiction program—it featured fantasy, horror, and gentle ironic drama as well. But Serling enjoyed using the sf genre to make philosophical points. "A Martian can say things," he once observed, "that a Republican or Democrat can't." Appropriately, then, many of the program's most memorable episodes featured alien beings as a sort of Greek chorus, commenting on human foibles and weaknesses. In "The Monsters Are Due on Maple Street," a pair of invaders wreak havoc on a small community by manipulating electricity—exposing man's self-

Rod Serling on his fame as a TV personality, 1960: "People see me on the street and they say, 'Why, we thought you were six foot one' or, 'We thought you looked like a movie actor.' And then they look at me and say, 'Why, this kid is five foot five and he's got a broken nose.' I photograph better than I look, and that's the problem."

destructive prejudices. In "Mr. Dingle, the Strong," Martians give a man superstrength and then watch him foolishly squander it on barroom exhibitions. In "The Eye of the Beholder," an alien woman who is beautiful by our standards is banished from her own society because, we learn, her peers—piglike humanoids—cosider her grotesque.

Today, almost thirty years after its premiere, "The Twilight Zone" remains the standard for television anthology programs because better than any other effort, it consistently captured the essence of science fiction. "Sure," Rod Serling once told a reporter, "there have been science fiction and fantasy shows before, but most of them were involved with gadgets or leprechauns. 'The Twilight Zone' is about people."

Serling poses with actress Inger Stevens, an occasional "TZ" star.

FLASHBACK

SERLING [Opening "The Monsters Are Due on Maple Street"]: "Maple Street, USA. Late summer. A tree-lined little road of front-porch gliders, barbecues, the laughter of children. … At the sound of the roar and the flash of light, it will be precisely 6:43 P.M. on Maple Street. … This is Maple Street on a late Saturday afternoon, in the last calm and reflective moment— before the monsters came."

SERLING [Closing same episode]: "The tools of conquest do not necessarily come with bombs and … fallout. There are weapons that are simply thoughts, prejudices—to be found only in the minds of men. For the record, prejudices can kill and suspicion can destroy, and a … frightened search for a scapegoat has a fall-out all its own—for the children, and the children yet unborn. The pity of it is that these things cannot be confined to the Twilight Zone."

VITAL STATS

POLL RESULTS:
- Second, 1452 pts.

PROGRAM INFO:
- CBS
- First show: Oct. 2, 1959
- Last show: Sept. 5, 1965
- 134 half-hour, 17 hour episodes

BACKGROUND: By the mid-'50s, Rod Serling was one television's most respected writers. In 1955, he won an Emmy for the teleplay of "Patterns," plus a full-time job writing for the prestigious show "Playhouse 90." The following year, he won another Emmy, for "Requiem for a Heavyweight." But as his reputation grew he became increasingly frustrated with his position. Sponsors kept undermining his work, changing its meaning by forcing fatuous changes. One of the show's advertisers, for example, was a cigarette company that forced Serling to eliminate the word *lucky* from a script—because Lucky cigarettes were manufactured by a competitor. And an insurance company refused to approve a script in which one of the characters committed suicide.

When Serling couldn't take it any more, he resigned. He began working on his own program, reasoning that if he buried his messages in science fiction and fantasy, he could sneak them past network censors and sponsors. In 1957, he rewrote an old script and presented it to CBS as a series pilot. The network rejected it, but an anthology series called "Desilu Playhouse" aired the program. It received so much positive response that CBS reconsidered. Serling was commissioned to write several more scripts, and one called "Where Is Everybody?" was finally accepted as "The Twilight Zone"'s first episode. Two years after he started, he had his own show.

THE WRITERS: Serling himself wrote the majority of "The Twilight Zone"'s episodes. In the first season, he composed 80 percent of them; by the fifth season, he was still responsible for half. Other prominent writers, established fantasists, included:
- **Richard Matheson**: Published his first story in 1950. Episodes include: "The Last Flight," "The Invaders," "Little Girl Lost."
- **Charles Beaumont**: Next to Serling, produced the most "Twilight Zone" scripts. Published his first story—"The Devil, You Say?"—in 1950. It was adapted into the episode "Printer's Devil." Epsiodes include: "A Nice Place to Visit," "The Howling Man," "Long Live Walter Jameson."

OPENING JITTERS

• For many viewers, the highlight of "The Twilight Zone" was Rod Serling's introduction, which began, "There is a fifth dimension beyond that which is known to man ..."

• Originally, the opening read, "There is a sixth dimension ...," until someone pointed out that there were only four dimensions (Serling had thought there were five).

• Surprisingly, Serling was not the original choice for narrator. Producers considered Westbrook Van Voorhis (rejected because he was "too pompous-sounding") and Orson Welles (they couldn't afford him) before Serling finally volunteered.

• The show's creator was so uptight about appearing on camera that he had to bring a supply of extra shirts with him every time they filmed; he sweated through one shirt per take.

"I'm not nearly as concerned with the money to be made on this show as I am with the quality of it."
—Rod Serling

• "When he had to do his lead-ins," one of Serling's directors recalled, "he would go through absolute hell. He would sweat and sputter and go pale. He was terribly ill at ease." Serling added: "Only my laundress knows how frightened I [really] am."

OH-H-H ZONE

Rod Serling was disappointed to learn that *twilight zone* was a term already in use with Air Force pilots; he thought he'd invented it. Actually, "TZ" wasn't even the first TV show to use the term. About a decade before Serling's first episode, the phrase was regularly used in "Tom Corbett" to describe the habitable area of a planet.

SPECIAL EFFECTS

"The Twilight Zone" succeeded without elaborate special effects. In the famous episode "Nightmare at 20,000 Feet," for example, the "monster's" shoes were showing. But when it came to more elaborate effects, Ser-

ling would have been in trouble if he hadn't had access to props from old films and other TV shows. Three examples:
• The sets in "Walking Distance" were actually redresses of those used in Judy Garland's 1944 musical, *Meet Me in St. Louis.*
• In "The Monsters Are Due on Maple Street," the aliens' outfits were from the classic 1956 science fiction film *Forbidden Planet.* The final shot (an alien ship flying through space) is from the same movie, rerun upside down and backwards.
• The crashed rocket ship in "Probe 7, Over and Out" was originally constructed for the "Outer Limits" episode "Specimen: Unkown." They sold it to Serling when they were done with it.

LAST ACT

The only "Twilight Zone" episode not made by Serling was *An Occurrence at Owl Creek Bridge*, a French film he discovered at a European film festival. He admired it so much that he decided to air it on his show.

Patricia Crowley, Robert Sterling, and Burgess Meredith in "The Printer's Devil." Along with Jack Klugman, Burgess Meredith made more appearances on "The Twilight Zone" than any other actor.

CRITICS' COMMENTS

ABOUT ITS APPEAL:

" 'Twilight Zone' was able to hook into the sort of primal fears that you can put in one sentence: the idea that maybe all of your machines really *can* think, that the nice-looking person sitting next to you is really the devil, that your little doll is really watching you."

—**Robert Bianco,**
Pittsburgh Press

" 'Twilight Zone' would take one fantastical element and introduce it into the familiar. ... For instance, in one program a little girl finds an entrance to another dimension in her room. Serling introduces an average family, living in an average house, and suddenly, this porthole— literally a porthole into the fantastic—appears ... A large audience could relate to that."

—**Jack Dann,** *SF Writer*

ABOUT THE PERFORMERS:

"They had wonderful actors: Robert Redford played Mr. Death; Ed Wynn did a couple of episodes that would break your heart; Art Carney was an alcoholic who was hired to be Santa Claus. A lot of the actors on the show later became familiar, like Klugman and Redford. But 'Twilight Zone' also gave people like Ed Wynn and Mickey Rooney, who weren't primarily known as dramatic actors, a chance to demonstrate their talents and play against type."

—**Ed Naha,**
The Science Fictionary

ABOUT THE STORIES:

"For me when science fiction works, it works on the level of human values, giving us a kind of strange prism through which to view our civilization. 'The Twilight Zone' did that."

—**Susan Paynter,**
Seattle Post-Intelligencer

"People would watch 'Twilight Zone' and at work the next day they'd still be talking about it, saying, 'My God, did you see that show last night?' How often does *that* happen with a TV show?"

—**C.J. Cherryh,** *SF Writer*

" 'Twilight Zone' showed that intelligent, literate anthology drama could be done on television. Science fiction was the veneer, but what Serling was really dealing with were little morality plays and well-crafted short stories. That's its legacy, and that's its value in television history."

—**Steve Sonsky,**
Miami Herald

Above: Burt Reynolds once played an author who conjured-up Shakespeare.
"At the time the show originally aired, the strongest part of 'The Twilight Zone' was the suggestion that someone could be living a standard 1960s urban lifestyle and suddenly turn a corner and be whisked into a total fantasy world—that anything was possible. 'Twilight Zone' sort of said, 'Well, you don't have to believe just what you see around you—there are other options.' "
—Marc Scott Zicree, *The Twilight Zone Companion*

THE OUTER LIMITS

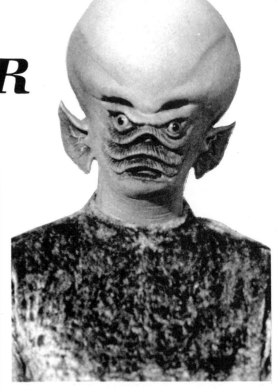

The Keeper of the Purple Twilight, a scout for an alien invasion force.

In 1957, Universal Pictures dusted off its library of old horror movies—Boris Karloff in *Frankenstein,* Bela Lugosi as Dracula, Lon Chaney as the Wolfman, etc.—and made them available to TV stations for the first time. Within a few years, they were on the small screen in every city in the country; a whole new generation of American kids got hooked on classic monsters. Commercialization wasn't far behind: In 1961, the Aurora Toy Corp. came out with plastic models of the Universal creatures and sold millions—and suddenly monster-mania was sweeping the United States. There were monster jokebooks, comics, games, wallets, cards, posters, shirts, slippers, hats. In 1962, "Monster Mash," a spoof by Bobby "Boris" Pickett, sold millions of records and hit #1 on the national charts.

Small wonder, then, that when ABC purchased the pilot of "Outer Limits" in 1963, it was more interested in pushing the horror elements of the show than encouraging its producers to develop its more thoughtful side. And to their credit, the producers gave the network what it was after—the creepiest creatures ever created for television: Zanti Misfits, giant ants with ugly human faces; Luminoids, the living rocks in the episode, "A Feasibility Study"; a one-eyed, flat-faced alien in "OBIT"; the grotesque Box Creature in "Do Not Open Until Doomsday."

But "The Outer Limits" has been saddled unfairly with a "monster" stigma. Actually, it may be the purest science fiction program ever presented on television. Each episode experimented with a form of the genre; there were no "fantasy" shows or expositions of regular characters. Stories were about journeys through other dimensions, time travel, strange scientific experiments. And in the best sf tradition, the science fictional elements were always subordinate to the message. Shows might *feature* monsters, but they were *about* people.

"The Zanti Misfits" literally asked the question, "What is society to do with those members who are a threat to it?" The harmless aliens in the episode "Chameleon" taught tolerance. "A man's survival can take many shapes," the narrator explained, "and the shape in which a man finds his humanity is not always a human one." In the classic "Architects of Fear," Robert Culp tried to trick the nations of Earth into peaceful coexistence and failed miserably. At the end, the Control Voice summed it up: "Scarecrows and magic and other fatal fears do not bring people closer together. There is no magic substitute for soft caring and hard work, for self-respect and mutual love."

Couched in purple prose and eerie, atmospheric cinematography, this kind of message was delivered weekly by fine actors, scary monsters, disembodied voices, and frustrated producers—all of whom felt, quite accurately, that even if the classic they were creating was overlooked in its own time, it would be properly appreciated in the future.

Joe Stefano, the producer credited with making "The Outer Limits" a superior series

FLASHBACK

THE CONTROL VOICE

[Introduction, "The Sixth Finger"]: "Where are we going? Life, the timeless, mysterious gift, is still evolving. What wonders—or terrors—does evolution hold in store for us in the next ten thousand years? In a million? In six million? Perhaps the answer lies in this old house in this old and misty valley. …"

[Closing, same episode]: "An experiment too soon, too swift, and yet may we still hope to discover a method by which, in one generation, the whole human race could be rendered intelligent, beyond hatred, or revenge, or the desire for power? Is that not, after all, the ultimate goal of evolution?"

"We now return control of your television set to you, until next week at this same time, when the Control Voice will take you to 'The Outer Limits.' "

VITAL STATS

POLL RESULTS:
• Third, 1105 pts.
PROGRAM INFO:
• Hour show, ABC
• First show: Sept.16, 1963
• Last show: Jan. 16, 1965
• 49 episodes

BACKGROUND: "The Outer Limits" started simply: A United Artists vice president suggested to a producer that they "cook up a TV series about science fiction." The producer, Leslie Stevens, was taken with the idea; he imagined creating a program that captured "the awe and mystery of the universe." But when he brought the concept to ABC's head of programming, Dan Melnick, the show's focus changed. "The one thing Dan urged me to do," Stevens recalled in *The Outer Limits: The Official Companion*, "was to put a monster in every show, and to put it on fast—within the first five minutes. Because ABC would regard the show as a monster show more than anything else." Stevens agreed, and Melnick commissioned a pilot entitled "Please Stand By."

THE PRODUCER: To produce the pilot, Stevens hired Joseph Stefano, who was known in Hollywood primarily as a screenwriter; his most famous work was Hitchcock's classic *Psycho*. Stefano had little experience with production and wasn't particularly fond of science fiction, but Stevens thought Stefano's presence would be attractive to ABC. He was right. "Joe would be the first person to say he hadn't produced his left shoe," Stevens commented. "There wasn't much for him to do except stand there and watch us film it ." But after the program was purchased by ABC, Stefano's presence made all the difference. He not only "came into his own as a producer," he brought the sensibility and integrity that made "The Outer Limits" worth watching. "I was hip to life, people, and situations," Stefano told David Schow. "I didn't know terribly much about being a producer, but with me, you never hire a producer; you hire Joe Stefano."

THE NAME: "Please Stand By" wasn't acceptable to ABC. They feared that an audience who only a year before had sat fearfully in front of their television sets watching the Cuban Missile Crisis unfold might be inclined to believe that another real emergency was taking place if an authoritative voice told them to "please stand by." So they changed the name to "The Outer Limits."

The Sand Shark from the episode "Invisible Enemy" was actually a hand puppet; the "sand" was really cork.

The monster from one of "The Outer Limits" ' classic episodes, "OBIT," a Perry Mason-like courtroom drama about an alien plot to demoralize Earth's population with telescreens. "Years later," says David Schow, "the OBIT mask turned up as a guest monster in an episode of 'The Munsters,' while the OBIT console ironically became the center of worldwide communications for Leo G. Carroll on 'The Man from UNCLE.' "

TERROR

It was by design, not accident, that "Outer Limits" scared the hell out of its audience. Creator Leslie Stevens gave the show's writers these instructions: "Enlightenment, education, provocation, and soul-moving are the end game of all drama, but to these must be added the experience of terror. It must, however, be *tolerable terror*. When the play has ended, when the Control Voice has returned to the viewer the control of his TV set, that willing victim of the terror must be able to relax and ... realize [that] what he feared during the story ... need not be feared should he walk out of his house and stroll a night street."

In "The Sixth Finger," Gwyllm Griffiths (David McCallum, right) evolved into the superintellect of the future. It was McCallum's first American TV appearance, and Joseph Stefano was so impressed that he wanted to star the actor in a new series. But ABC rejected the idea because McCallum was "too short." The following year, "The Man From UNCLE" made McCallum a superstar—on NBC.

CRITICS' COMMENTS

ON ITS POINT OF VIEW:
"One thing I like about ... 'The Outer Limits' is that it had a moral compass. It wasn't riding the fence, it was saying there *is* a right and a wrong in life, and you're either on the side of the people who are addressing the problem, or you're part of the problem. You rarely get that in television."

—**Marc Scott Zicree,**
The Twilight Zone
Companion

ABOUT THE ACTING:
" 'The Outer Limits' had that New York style to it; these were real actors—stage-type actors, not TV personnae—and that gave their stories a little more grit and texture. Every week you'd see people who were good at what they did, even if they just played small parts; guys might play security guards and have only two lines ... but they were *somebody*."

—**Peter Farrell,**
The Oregonian

ABOUT THE OPENING:
" 'The Outer Limits,' with its introduction, had a *feel* that some outside force was taking over the TV. It *captured*."
—**Fritz Leiber,** *SF Writer*

"It took me years to get control of my TV set again."
—**Pat Murphy,** *SF Writer*

ABOUT THE MONSTERS:
" 'The Outer Limits' monsters were very uneven. They had a very low budget, and technology wasn't very advanced at the time. But ... they were able to do things with light and shadow and mood to convey suspense or terror—and make a monster work better than just by using special effects. This wasn't only clever, it actually improved the quality of the show. They couldn't do anything about making the special effects better ... so they got creative."

—**Margaret Weiner,**
Fantasy News

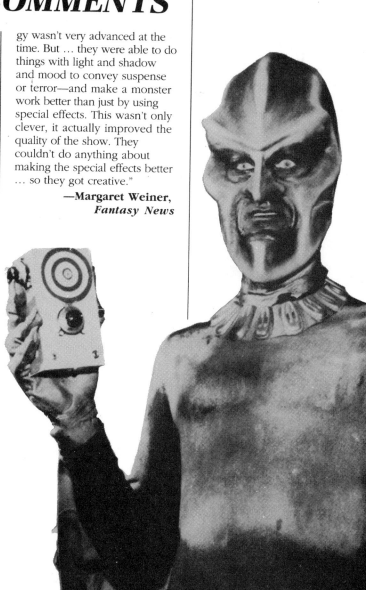

"It was a fantastic show in every sense of the word. ... They had great creepy monsters, wonderful music, terrific eye-catching openings. ... I like the film noir look of it, the black and white spookiness. In fact, it was one of the few television shows ever to have a consistent look, week after week."
—Tom Shales, *Washington Post*

THE HITCHHIKER'S GUIDE TO THE GALAXY

"The Hitchhiker's Guide to the Galaxy" debuted as a Sunday night BBC radio show on March 8, 1978. At first, hardly anyone listened. But as the series wore on, it attracted a cult following; fans discussed it, quoted it, passed tapes of it around at science fiction conventions. By the last episode, people who'd missed the first part of the series were clamoring to hear it from the beginning—so the BBC ran the whole thing a second time. And then a third time. And a fourth. It became a national sensation. The BBC commissioned a second series, and when Douglas Adams converted his scripts into a novel, the book rocketed to the top of the English bestseller lists.

Today there are two "Hitchhiker's" record albums, one single, four books, a stage play, a movie treatment, a published collection of the original radio scripts, and a seven-part television adaptation that somehow managed to transform the purely auditory humor of the original into a spectacle that many people feel is the funniest science fiction show ever created.

The show is part satire, part fantasy, part wordplay. It's a science fiction version of *Alice in Wonderland*—a Mad Tea Party attended by one wide-eyed innocent named Arthur Dent, and a host of frighteningly illogical creatures who are quite convinced they're perfectly rational. In fact, they all think *Arthur's* the crazy one.

In *Alice*, for example, Tweedledee and Tweedledum recite nonsensical poetry. In "The Hitchhiker's Guide," it's the Vogons—who actually *torture* people with their horrible verse. There's the philosopher, Vroomfondel, who insists that he doesn't have to be anybody he doesn't want to be—not even himself. "We demand rigidly defined areas of doubt and uncertainty," he declares. There are two pandimensional beings of vast intellect, who disguise themselves as rodents to run experiments on human beings; they like to run through mazes and drop

The original American edition of *The Hitchhiker's Guide*.

dead, to see how people will react. Then there's Marvin the Paranoid Android, the creation of inept designers who gave him all the wrong personality traits. He's convinced that everything and everyone is against him; he's a hypochondiac; he's suicidal. "Don't mind me," he comments at one point. "No one ever does."

Besides wacky characters and a plethora of puns, the real genius of the show is in its visual adaptations. The BBC is notorious for cheap special effects; but they actually spent money on this show, and Adams and co. made extremely creative use of it. When it's necessary to refer to the *Guide*, for example, computer animation converts the viewer's TV screen *into* the book. And when there's a space war in the story, viewers find themselves suddenly watching a video game. "This is, of course impossible," the narrator interjects several times during the show—just making sure that the audience doesn't lose sight of the cosmic joke. And for the most part, we never do.

Douglas Adams turned "The Hitchhiker's Guide" into a series that ended with the fourth book, *So Long, and Thanks for the Fish.*

FLASHBACK

MARVIN [woefully] : "I think you should know I'm feeling very depressed."

FORD [Trying to explain the concept of hyper-space]: "It's very unpleasantly like being drunk."

ARTHUR: "What's so unpleasant about being drunk?"

FORD: "Ask a glass of water."

NARRATOR [describing the great days of the Galactic Empire]: "Men were real men. Women were real women. Small furry creatures from Alpha Centauri were real small furry creatures from Alpha Centauri."

VITAL STATS

POLL RESULTS:
• Fourth, 865 pts.
PROGRAM INFO:
• Hour show. Originally, BBC
• First shown: 1983
• 7 episodes

TIME: Begins in the present, jumps forward to the end of the Universe, retreats two million years into Earth's past.

PLACE: All over the Galaxy.

BACKGROUND: The electronic book, *The Hitchhiker's Guide to the Galaxy*, is the standard repository for information on the Universe. Unfortunately, it's wildly inaccurate, so it needs constant updating. Ford Prefect, a field researcher updating the entry on Earth, gets stuck on our planet for fifteen years and barely escapes its impending destruction (to make way for a hyperspace bypass) by thumbing a ride on a UFO. He saves his human friend, Arthur Dent, as well. Meanwhile, ex-galactic President Zaphod Beeblebrox has stolen the spaceship *Heart of Gold* and is looking for the lost planet Magrathea, whose business is building other planets. And a pair of pandimensional beings that look exactly like two white mice are searching for the Ultimate Question to Life, the Universe and Everything. They already know the Ultimate Answer—it's 42.

Simon Jones, aka Arthur Dent.

MAIN CAST:
• **Arthur Dent** (Simon Jones): Typical Briton; the last survivor of Earth. Wanders through the Universe in a state of total befuddlement, trying to find a good cup of tea. He's the only one who might possibly know the Ultimate Question.
• **Zaphod Beeblebrox** (Mark Wing-Davies): Two-headed ex-confidence trickster, part-time Galactic President. Unreliable, greedy, cowardly.
• **Ford Prefect** (David Dixon): Field researcher for the *Guide*—which means he spends a lot of time in bars. Arthur's devoted friend .
• **Trillian** (Sandra Dickenson): Born Trisha McMillan on Earth, she was picked up at a party by Zapphod Beeblebrox. Now she pilots the starship *Heart of Gold*, which is powered by improbablility drive.
• **Marvin, the Paranoid Android** (Stephen Moore): Manic-depressive robot with a brain the size of a planet. Has a constant pain in his diodes.
• **Vogons**: Fat, ugly, green. Write the worst poetry in the Galaxy. Not evil—just officious, bureaucratic, and sadistic.
• **Golgafrinchians**: Middle management people, ad execs, telephone sanitizers who were thrown off their home planet because they were useless. The human race's direct ancestors.

REVERSE EFFECTS

• When the actors and crew filmed "Hitchhiker's Guide," they didn't know much about special effects and were proud of the quality they were able to achieve. "But when I got over to this country," says Simon Jones, "fans would come up and say, 'Oh, we loved the special effects—they're so cheap, so tacky.' So I had to change my story. I'd say, 'Oh yes, we meant to do it that way.' "

• Actually, "Hitchhiker's Guide" was almost cancelled immediately after the first episode was shot, because of the *"high cost"* of the effects. Shocked BBC executives put the project on hold for a month before reluctantly deciding it was worth the money.

MARV

Marvin the Paranoid Android started out as a one-scene joke and became "Hitchhiker's" most popular character. He was also the hardest to adapt from radio. First, there was the design: "We didn't know if he should look permanently depressed," says special effects man Jim Francis, "or if he should be programmed to be depressed but look normal on the outside...In the end, we went through nine or ten different designs." The other problem was the robot suit itself. Francis wanted to avoid any resemblance to C3P0, so instead of rubber joints for Marvin, he opted for mechanical ones. Unfortunately, that meant the actor who played the robot couldn't get his arms into the costume. It took a while to solve the problem. "The final joint...was a sort of sliding shutter with a gap underneath. It's not easy to make a human arm do a mechanical movement inside a box," Francis concludes.

PEOPLE-WATCHING

• **Douglas Adams** actually makes an appearance in the second episode of the show. While the narrator is discussing money, Adams is seen withdrawing some from the bank, throwing it away, taking off his clothes on a beach, and then walking into the water naked.

• **Peter Davison**, the sixth Dr. Who, made a guest appearance as The Dish of the Day. He probably did it because his wife played Trillian.

• **David Prowse**, who played Darth Vader, also had a role in "Hitchhiker." He played a bodyguard for Plutonium rock 'n' roller Hotblack Desiado

• **Shootie and Bang-Bang**, the two enlightened liberal galactic cops who shot people and then agonized about it with their girlfriends were actually takeoffs on "Starsky and Hutch."

Zaphod on camera. Zaphod's second head was a radio controlled model perched on actor Mark Wing-Davies' shoulder. It "wasn't as effective in the show as it was in rehearsal," says Douglas Adams. "Every time something went wrong with his head...you'd have to spend an hour taking it apart and putting it back together again and we didn't have that hour. So we just sort of fudged it as best we could." (Photos above and right, © 1983 Kevin Davies)

"The real appeal of the show is that it takes such prosaic and mundane things and translates them into galactic terms. The idea of bulldozing earth, for example, to make way for intergalactic projects. And the 'Dish of the Day' in the Restaurant At the End of the Universe, which is not only a dish, but a dish that talks to you, and tells you which parts of it are especially tasty.
—R.D. Heldenfels, *Schenectady Gazette*

CRITICS' COMMENTS

ABOUT HUMOR IN SF:
"I once read that Woody Allen's vision of the future in *Sleeper* is as valid as Stanley Kubrick's in *2001*, and that's probably true...That's why I like 'Hitchhiker's Guide'—it's one of the few pieces of science fiction with a bizarre sense of humor."
—**Noel Holston,**
***Minneapolis Star
and Tribune***

"Science fiction is pretty self-inflated, and if you've read a lot of standard science fiction stories, which basically all say, 'You, a 13-year old pimply bookworm hold the secrets to the universe,' 'The Hitchhiker's Guide' is kind of funny. You have to have a familiarity with the cliches of science fiction, and a certain affection for them, to be amused by it."
—**Michael Cassutt,**
SF / TV writer

**ABOUT THE
CHARACTERS:**
"Arthur Dent was sort of an Everyman. He's just the Englishman abroad. Very far abroad, but abroad nonetheless."
—**Elizabeth Anne
Scarborough, *SF Writer***

"What characters? They're just comic concepts. There's no characterization in this show. There are continuing characters, but they're written very large. It's like saying, 'Tell me about the characters in "Abbot and Costello." ' "
—**Bill Warren,**
Look to the Skies

ABOUT SPECIAL EFFECTS:
" 'Hitchhiker's Guide' showed that science fiction is more than special effects—that science fiction, to work really well, depends more on good writing than good technology."
—**Ed Siegel**,
Boston Globe

"The purpose of special effects is to make the viewer see that which doesn't exist in the present world....[but] when you get to a show like...'Hitchhiker's Guide' where we all know they're just horsing around, the special effects don't need to be anything more than horsing around."
—**Robert Silverberg,**
SF Writer

DOCTOR WHO

"Dr. Who," now in its twenty-fourth year, is the science fiction program that refuses to die—the low-budget English kids' show that has outlived every other network program in history—British *or* American—by converting its weaknesses into strengths. When the producers had no special effects budget, they concentrated on story lines and encouraged the audience to chuckle at the cheap visuals. When the original star got too old and ill to continue, they hired a new one—and told the audience that the character had transformed himself. When the audience was tired of the show's educational orientation, producers sent the Doctor off into space to fight with alien beings.

The result is that over the course of the show's long run, "Dr. Who"'s writers and producers have developed a uniquely flexible format that enables them to do whatever they want with the main character. Only his name and avocation (traveling around through time and space in a police box) are fixed; the rest is totally unpredictable. He can go anywhere, do anything, meet anybody. Dr. Who and his companions have traveled with Marco Polo; they've been involved in the Gunfight at the OK Corral; they've visited the planet Peladon, a medieval society in space; they've traveled to prehistoric Earth to witness the beginning of life; they journeyed to Telos, one of the homes of the Cybermen. They've been to literally hundreds of different planets and time periods.

But it's not just the traveling that has made "Dr. Who" America's #1 underground cult TV show. To "Whovians," the Doctor is as fascinating as his destinations, a complex character with only one predictable heroic trait—bravery. And even *that* he uses sparingly; 99 percent of the time, the Doctor would rather talk (or think) his way out of a jam than do battle.

Fans are also attracted by the fact that none of the various Doctors takes himself too seriously. For

Fans love to read about "Dr. Who." In addition to numerous magazines covering the show, like the ones above, there have been over 1,500 books written about it—more than any other TV program in history. (Magazines © Movie Publishers' Distributors)

every power the Time Lord acquires, he acquires an equal weakness. Tom Baker's popular Dr. Who is all-powerful, for example, but he's also a cosmic blunderer. "Well, I can't get everything right," he tells Romana in one episode. "Just *something*," she replies, "would be a help."

In an anthology, producers can do anything they like, but they can't have a regular character to do it with. In a continuing series, there are regular characters but the action is limited by the show's setting. "Dr. Who" has the best of both, and employs writers who know how to have fun with that freedom. In an episode called "The City of Death," for example, a group of thieves are planning to steal the Mona Lisa. Just a normal adventure show? Well, the gang is actually headed by a monster from outer space, who is financing his time travel experiments by stealing art treasures. Where else on TV can viewers expect to see something so off the wall? Not on cop shows like "Starsky and Hutch." Or space operas like "Star Trek." And it's too silly for a serious anthology like "The Twilight Zone." That kind of endearing insanity is the exclusive property of "Dr. Who"—which is why fans are *still* watching it.

VITAL STATS

The Doctor is always accompanied by at least one companion—usually an attractive female. And for a pet he's got K-9, the robot dog. (Photo © Susan Moore)

FLASHBACK

DR. WHO: "Homo sapiens— what an inventive, invincible species! It's only a few million years since they crawled out of the mud and learned to walk. Puny, defenseless bipeds, they've survived flood, famine, and plague. They've survived cosmic wars and holocausts. And now, here they are, out among the stars, waiting to begin a new life, ready to outsit eternity. They're indomitable … indomitable."

DR. WHO: "I am citizen of the universe, and a gentleman to boot."

DR. WHO: "Have you ever thought what it's like to be exiled, to be wanderers in space and time?"

POLL RESULTS:
• Fifth, 792 pts.
PROGRAM INFO:
• Half-hour show. PBS
• First show: Nov. 23, 1963 (England)
• Last show: Still in production

BACKGROUND: Dr. Who is a Time Lord, of the Prydonian chapter, a race of beings who inhabit the planet Gallifrey. Time Lords have almost complete mastery of time and space—but abide by a strict non-interference policy. The Doctor found this annoying, so he stole a Tardis and fled the planet—and now roams freely around the Galaxy with his companions. As a Time Lord, he has the ability to regenerate up to twelve times. At the moment, he's in his seventh form. For each regeneration, his personality and appearance change.

THE TARDIS: (Time and Relative Dimension in Space). The Doctor's vehicle, a type 40 TT Capsule, larger on the inside than the outside. Can travel anywhere in time and space, but has been patched and repaired so much it's unreliable. Should be able to disguise itself as an inconspicuous object in its surroundings, but since it's broken, it now must remain a London Police Box, ca. A.D. 1960.

THE DOCTORS:
• **Doctor #1** (William Hartnell): A middle-aged (739 years), cranky, grandfatherish man. Equally arrogant and brilliant.
• **Doctor #2** (Patrick Troughton): Younger man (in his mid-400s), with an impish sense of humor. Seems weak and cowardly, but uses his penetrating mind rather than fighting to defeat foes.
• **Doctor #3** (Jon Pertwee): Silver-haired adventurer, into Venusian Aikido, fast cars, and action.
• **Doctor #4** (Tom Baker): Curly-mopped, long-scarved Bohemian with an engaging sense of humor and contagious smile. Extremely unpredictable.
• **Doctor #5** (Peter Davison): Youngest-looking, with an air of confusion and fallibility. Seems nervous and ill at ease.
• **Doctor #6** (Colin Baker): Arrogant, smug, ingratiating, but willing to risk his life for the common good. A nonchalant fighter.
• **Doctor #7** (Sylvester McCoy): At this writing, he's too new to know.

THE COMPANIONS: Dr. Who never travels alone. His partners include **Susan Foreman**, **Jamie McCrimmon**, **Leela**, **K-9**, **Romana**, **Adric**, **Peri**, etc.

THE VILLAINS: Include the **Daleks**, the **Cybermen**, the **Master**, and before they were converted to allies, the **Ice Warriors**.

Colin Baker was the sixth Doctor. "Dr. Who" is a cult program in over 50 countries. One exception: for some reason, "Dr. Who" has still never been seen in France.

Jon Pertwee, the third Doctor, was one of the most popular—although it was Tom Baker who garnered the best ratings in England—an audience of around 14 million.

TARDIS TROUBLE

The Doctor travels the universe in his TARDIS—Time and Relative Dimension in Space— which looks suspiciously like a British phone booth. Actually, the original plans called for the TARDIS to change appearances and camouflage itself wherever Dr. Who landed. If he landed in ancient Rome, for example, the TARDIS would look like a marble column. The first episode took place in London, so the TARDIS took the form of a common London sight—a "police box." After it was built, the producers realized they'd blown half their budget on it and couldn't afford to keep changing it—so it remained a phone booth for the entire series.

BORN AGAIN

Dr. Who's unique ability to regenerate was born out of necessity when William Hartnell, the aging first Doctor Who, became ill. He'd always had trouble remembering his lines, but now he began missing shows as well. The BBC gave script editor Jerry Davis and producer Innes Lloyd two choices: Try someone new, or cancel the show. "Dr. Who" was too successful to cancel, so the two men came up with a wild idea for explaining a new star: The Doctor has the ability to change shape and personality. The BBC figured there was no harm done—if the idea didn't work, the show would be dropped. But it worked; two decades later, the Doctor has had seven different personalities, and is still regenerating.

FUSS-BUDGET

"Dr. Who" has never had much of a special effects budget to work with. In 1963, for example, the Daleks were built with a total budget of $800. The script called for six of them, but the producers could afford only four—so they had to use two cardboard cut-outs with photos of the Daleks pasted on to give the appearance that there were a half dozen on the set. By the Tom Baker years, the special effects budget was up to around $4,000 per episode, a 500 percent increase, but still minuscule by American standards.

THEY'RE HERE

"Dr. Who" was originally planned as an educational/entertainment show in which the Doctor's travels—inspired by H.G. Wells' *The Time Machine*—would expose children to history. Aliens and monsters were absolutely forbidden. But every time producer Verity Lambert sneaked in the Daleks, the ratings went up. So creator Sidney Newman finally gave up and let the BEMs (Bug-Eyed Monsters) take over.

CRITICS' COMMENTS

ABOUT WHO'S WHO:

" 'Dr. Who' is the Howard Hesseman of futuristic fiction."
—**Peter Farrell,** *The Oregonian*

"To remain a kids' hero, he has had to exhibit a little of that clownish eccentricity that makes it OK for children to associate with a grown-up."
—**C.J. Cherryh,** *SF Writer*

ABOUT DIFFERENT DOCTORS:

"The Doctor you prefer depends on the Doctor you started with. You accept the actor who plays the doctor when you began watching the show, and the rest seem like replacements. With American fans, this is mostly Tom Baker, of course. He was the only one who was widely syndicated over here for a long time; the rest followed on the heels of his success."
—**Gordon Javna,** *60s!*

"I loved William Hartnell, the first Doctor. You could never be sure with him. He could be very stern and demanding, or he could be very indulgent. Actually, he was very much like one's parents, who sometimes lay down the law, sometimes let you do what you like. He was cranky and touchy, but he had some magic about him that none of the other Dr. Who's had."
—**John Peel,** *The Dr. Who Files*

"I liked the third one, Jon Pertwee ... because he had a certain sense of class—almost British elegance. He was reassuring, older, wiser, yet James Bondish enough to do the 'Dr. Who' equivalent of karate chops."
—**Walter Podrazik,** *Watching TV*

ABOUT THE EFFECTS:

"They have some of the tackiest special effects you'll ever see—like a serpent that suddenly expands and looks like something left over from 'Beany and Cecil.' But by then you're hooked enough on the story to go, 'Ok it's stupid, but I forgive it.' "
—**R.D. Heldenfels,** *Schenectady Gazette*

ABOUT THE SCRIPTS:

"You so rarely see anything that really tries to be different, that tries to break out, on television. On that basis alone, 'Dr. Who' is a kick. But the strong point of the show is the writing and the imagination that went into it. It was written by people willing to take a flight of imagination—people who didn't look to copy other forms." —**Rick Du Brow,** *L.A. Herald Examiner*

"It's just damn good writing ... which is typical of British TV in general, where the writers are more important than the actors, producers, or directors."
—**Bob Foster,** *San Mateo Times*

"One of the appealing things about 'Dr. Who' is the fact that they get along with $1.37 special effects; the zippers do show, occasionally. It takes me back to the early days of live television, when if you looked hard enough, you could see the strings holding the spaceships up. There was sort of amateurish 'roll on the floor and have a good time with it' quality about them. That's what 'Dr. Who' has. "
—Robert Jordan, *SF Writer*
(Photo © Susan Moore)

AMAZING STORIES

Sid Caesar starred in the episode called "Mr. Magic."

From the beginning, "Amazing Stories" was more than just another TV series; it was an historic event, a video dream. "The most eagerly awaited anthology series ever," one magazine called it.

"Amazing Stories" came equipped with the best of everything. It had the biggest budget in TV history; it had world-famous film directors; it had first-rate film actors; and best of all, it was masterminded by Steven Spielberg, the director/producer responsible for some of the most popular science fiction and fantasy box office hits in history. The man who created *E.T.*, *Close Encounters*, and *Poltergeist* was bringing his magic back to TV.

Unfortunately, things didn't work out as planned. "Amazing Stories" was largely ignored by audiences, and only reluctantly endorsed by critics. Even in this poll, while they overwhelmingly named it as one of the best sf programs ever, critics expressed serious reservations about the show.

The strength of "Amazing Stories" is unquestionably its visual appeal. Given the resources, Spielberg pushed the boundaries of this visual medium beyond anything it had ever known. "Amazing"'s production values were unsurpassed in television history. Each episode had the quality of a feature film, and its special effects were both charming and stunning. In one episode, Sid Caesar played a magician whose card tricks no longer worked. Then, in a marvelous moment, his cards took off by themselves, flying over the audience, even spelling out his name. In another, a crippled World War II bomber suddenly sprouted cartoon tires, enabling it to land. And in the premiere, a locomotive plowed through a house in such convincing fashion that it seemed authentic.

But there was a flip side. Many critics were troubled that "the stories and characters never amounted to anything." In the locomotive episode, for example, the characters are never developed beyond one-dimensional stereotypes: The grandfather, an ex-engineer, is a typically lovable old man; the grandson is an earnest youngster devoted to the grandfather; and the parents are well-meaning grown-ups who've lost their sense of wonder. The entire plot can be stated in two sentences: An old man explains to his grandson that a ghost train will arrive to take him back to a terrible moment in his past and let him live it over again. The parents think he's crazy and almost prevent him from accomplishing his task; but sure enough, a train arrives in their living room and whisks Grandpa away. That's all there is to it. Unlike "The Twilight Zone," there's no point, no engaging statement about human existence. It's just an amusing little tale that anyone could tell.

Nonetheless, Spielberg deserves enormous credit for trying. Experiments are rare in the play-it-safe world of television, and every one is valuable. Only time will tell just *how* valuable the contributions of "Amazing Stories" are. Certainly, it has permanently raised television's visual standards.

Actor John Cryer gets more than he bargained for in "Miscalculation."

FLASHBACK

"Calling it television's *Heaven's Gate* would be something of an exaggeration, but there is no disguising the fact that the very expensive—$800,000-$1,000,000 per half-hour episode—'Amazing Stories' has not lived up to the expectations of either NBC or a good many viewers. Promising a series of 'wonderment, fantasy, irony, and comedy,' Steven Spielberg, the excecutive producer, has delivered a spotty skein of cliches, sentimentality, and ordinary hokum."
—*The New York Times*, **October 1985**

" 'Amazing Stories,' Steven Spielberg confided to one reporter, was "my elephant burial ground for ideas that will never make it to the movie screen."

VITAL STATS

POLL RESULTS:
• Sixth , 688 pts.
PROGRAM INFO:
• Half-hour show. NBC
• First show: Oct. 6, 1985
• Last show: Still airing on cable
• 44 episodes

BACKGROUND: In 1968, Stephen Spielberg made a twenty-three–minute film called "Amblin'. " "I've been in love with the short-subject business ever since," he told *Rolling Stone* magazine. "Before television and feature films, I was a short-film maker." That may be the reason he announced to MCA head Sidney Sheinberg, in 1985, "I want to do an anthology show." "Which led," said one critic, "to an NBC deal faster than you can say 'deficit financing.' "

ANTHOLOGY BREAKTHROUGHS: "Amazing Stories" wasn't Spielberg's first experience with an anthology show; his debut as a director came on an episode of "Rod Serling's Night Gallery." But "Amazing Stories" broke new ground in many ways: most of the story ideas were generated by Spielberg himself; the budget—an average of $900,000 per show—was the largest for any half-hour program in history; Spielberg got an unprecedented two-year, forty-four episode committment from NBC; and it was the first anthology series that functioned as a vehicle for directors rather than producers or actors. "It's been interesting for me to see how interpretive directing could take [my] stories to many different places, very often away from my concept," Spielberg said prior to the show's premiere. "But I believe in giving directors a free hand. This is a director's series, not a producer's series.

The men fight their way up from the beach in "No Day at the Beach," directed by Lesli Linka Glatter. Glatter, one of the little-known directors selected by Spielberg to participate in his experiment, had received an Oscar nomination for a short film entitled "Tales of Meeting and Parting," but had never worked with a large budget before "Amazing Stories." It was mind-boggling. In fact, she once joked, the budget of her acclaimed short "was about enough to pay for 7-Up on the ['Amazing Stories'] set."

Kathryn Borowitz turns away from the image of her husband (played by Jeffrey Jonas) staring out from the computer screen in "The Eternal Mind," directed by Michael Riva.

> *"I did not want to enter into television unless I got a two-year guarantee."*
> —Steven Spielberg

THE NAME

The name "Amazing Stories" is special to science fiction buffs. In the days when the chief source of sf was twenty-five cent pulp magazines, "Amazing Stories" was consistently the best. Buck Rogers, for example, was introduced to the world in a 1929 issue of *Amazing Stories*. In fact, the magazine's first editor was Hugo Gernsback, the man responsible for coining the term "science fiction" in the first place.

THE DIRECTORS

Spielberg's reputation, charisma, and budget attracted directors who had otherwise avoided working on TV, including Martin Scorsese, Tobe Hooper, and Peter Hyams. It also tempted Clint Eastwood and Burt Reynolds, box office idols who had once starred in their own series, to return to the medium as directors. Perhaps most important, Spielberg's privileged status enabled him to offer little-known directors a chance to stretch out in the big leagues. For people like Phil Joanou, Mickey Moore, Don Petrie, and Lesli Linka Glatter, "Amazing Stories" was a rare gift.

CRITICS' COMMENTS

ABOUT THE EFFORT:

"I give Spielberg a lot of credit for his willingness to experiment with 'Amazing Stories.' He gave a lot of young talent an opportunity to show what they could do. And he also hired a lot of established talent to do things that they don't normally do—people like Martin Scorcese, or Clint Eastwood, who don't usually work in TV. It's exciting when that kind of thing happens to television."

—**Michael Duffy,**
Detroit Free Press

"I don't think they've been all good or all bad, but I think they've been ambitious attempts, and things like that should be encouraged on television. It has some basic problems—like, Spielberg used filmmakers who didn't know how to make television....I wish he'd gone out and found people who make television instead, and said, 'Here's a pile of money. Let's see what we can do.' "

—**Michael Hill,**
Baltimore Evening Sun

ABOUT THE LOOK:

"I've been waiting for a show like 'Amazing Stories' to come along and expand TV's visual frontiers. It's about time."

—**Margaret Weimer**
Fantasy News

"It's one of the best—if not *the*

Charles Durning looks at Gregory Wagrowski as he passes through his nightmare in "You Gotta Believe Me," directed by Kevin Reynolds.

"The scripts from 'Amazing Stories' are like modern day fairy tales—what Hans Christian Anderson might write if he was alive today and used a word processor. Even when the endings are predictable, the special effects make the series worthwhile. This is a rare example of a series that worked even after the producer had a two-year network commitment."

—Barry Garron, *Kansas City Star*

best—looking shows on television. It's a half-hour movie; it doesn't come off like TV most of the time. The production values are so high that you get the feeling you're watching something more important than a TV show."

—**"Weird Al" Yankovic,**
Singer/Actor

"Yes, the special effects were good—but don't forget that each show cost around a million dollars. They *should* have had a few special effects for those prices."

—**R.K. Shull,**
Indianapolis News

ABOUT THE CONTENT:

" 'Amazing Stories' is … Spielberg's pet project, and he supposedly came up with all the ideas for the stories himself. But I don't think Spielberg or *anybody* is capable of coming up with a smashing new science fiction idea every week. There are tens, if not hundreds, of thousands of already-published stories to choose from—of which there are many, many brilliant ones worthy of being adapted for a TV audience. … It seems like an egotrip to me that Spielberg thought he could produce the equivalent of the best of the science fiction genre."

—**George Alec Effinger,**
SF Writer

"This is one of the worst ten shows of all time, in any catagory. It's a disappointment every week. You tune in and expect something, and get nothing. … It's incredibly over-cute and over-produced and over-acted … with primitive premises about little things that children could make up around a campfire.

—**Tom Shales,**
Washington Post

MORK AND MINDY

Most people forget that "Mork and Mindy," in addition to being a generally brilliant sitcom, was a science fiction show. In fact, Mork was easily the most endearing alien ever to grace the small screen. Unlike the frequent interplanetary visitors on other programs, he wasn"t a bit hostile to our—or any other—civilization. He was like a child: ingenuous, eager, excited. He just wanted to get along with his neighbors and eventually understand humans well enough to feel comfortable on Earth.

Of course, one might question whether an alien character was essential to "Mork and Mindy." The program relied on a classic "fish out of water" theme, after all. Would it have made any difference if the hero was from Yugoslavia instead of outer space? You bet. Mork's complete innocence about even the simplest details of human existence, captured stunningly by Robin Williams, was what made the show effective. Mork was believable when he talked to potted plants, sat on his head, drank water with his finger. In one episode, Mork was aghast to discover eggs "imprisoned" in Mindy's refrigerator. On Ork the eggs would have been spaceships, so our hero decided to "liberate" them. Hurling them into the air, he cried, "Fly, little brothers, fly." The horrified look on his face as they splatted on the floor was one of the series' funniest moments.

"Mork" exploited several classic elements of science fiction. The juxtaposition of an alien with humans was used to examine our habits and values. And in a backhanded way, the show speculated on the nature of extraterrestrial life. "Maybe aliens aren't not so scary," it said; "maybe they're just as wacky as we are." And finally, Mork's closing reports to his home planet were explicit comments on Earth life—from an alien viewpoint. They weren't subtle, but they were charming when delivered by Robin Williams. "Well Orson," he might explain, "I know it's hard to understand, but to a lot of people, *things* are more important than other humans...

They have so much to learn."

One thing we did learn was that Robin Williams is an incredible talent. It was clear that no one could play an alien being more convincingly, with or without heavy makeup and scaly claws—especially in the beginning when Mindy was at her most bewildered, trying to cope with the lunatic creature living in her apartment.

Because of "Mork," Williams developed an instant reputation as the funniest, most off-the-wall comedian in America. So in retrospect, the most appropriate milestone of "Mork and Mindy" may be that Robin—as Mork, the delightful wacko from outer space who got everything backward—became the only male ever to give birth on TV. Nanoo, nanoo.

"I think it is a mistake," said Pam Dawber in 1980, "to lead people on and suggest there is sex or romance between Mork and Mindy. There isn't." But later in the show, they were married.

FLASHBACK

MORK: "Why do they call it rush hour when nothing moves?"

MINDY [using Exidor in a scheme to fool immigration officials]: "Do you remember what you're supposed to do?"
EXIDOR: "Certainly. I'm to be dignified, respectable, and just as crazy as the rest of the people in this world."
MORK: "Do you think you can do that?"
EXIDOR: "Oh sure. I'm great at impressions."

MINDY: "How do they say 'Thank you' in your language."
MORK [beaming]: "We spit."

Mindy tells Mork that on Earth, it's not polite to sit on your face.
MORK: "Then why did God put it there?"

VITAL STATS

POLL RESULTS:
•Seventh, 657 pts.
PROGRAM INFO:
•Half-hour show. ABC
•First show: Sept. 14, 1978
•Last show: June 10, 1982
•104 episodes

BACKGROUND: Ork is an advanced world bleems and bleems away from Earth. Its inhabitants have long observed our planet and its confusing customs from a distance, and have now decided to learn about it firsthand. So Mork is sent here as their observer. This is not necessarily an honor; he's been making fun of Ork's leader, Orson, and the big cheese wants him off the planet. Arriving in Boulder, Colorado, in a giant eggshell, Mork befriends a young student named Mindy McConnell and manages to move in with her (Mindy isn't sure how). It starts out as a platonic relationship, but after living together for a few years they fall in love and marry. Then they honeymoon on Ork, where Mork discovers he's pregnant. He lays an egg, and their middle-aged son, Mearth—who will grow younger each year—hatches from it.

MAIN CAST:
•**Mork from Ork** (Robin Williams): Frenetic, innocent, curious, apparently crazy. His father was an eye dropper, his mother a test tube. Sent to Earth to gather information quietly, he can't remain inconspicuous. He sits on his head, drinks with his finger, fights by "holitacker," using his fingers to duel. His powers include the ability to speed up his age or slow down time.
•**Mindy McConnell** (Pam Dawber): Liberal All-American girl. The only daughter of Fred McConnell. Studied journalism at University of Colorado, became a TV reporter after graduation.

SUPPORTING CAST:
•**Fred McConnell** (Conrad Janis): Mindy's excitable father, owner of Fred's Music Store.
•**Cora Hudson** (Elizabeth Kerr): Mindy's swinging grandmother, addicted to rock music and motorcycles.
•**Exidor** (Robert Donner): A harmless schizophrenic UFO prophet who thinks Mork is crazy.
•**Mearth** (Jonathan Winters): M. and M.'s child, calls Mork "Mommy" and Mindy "Shoe"; middle-aged, overweight. Will grow down instead of up.
•**Orson** (Ralph James): Orkan leader referred to by Mork as "Your Immenseness"; is heard every week, but never appears.

Jonathan Winters was Robin Williams's boyhood idol. "I must have been about eight or nine," Williams recalled in 1978, "and my parents would let me stay up whenever Jonathan Winters was on with Jack Paar. Jonathan is the Muhammad Ali of comedy, the greatest. He's like helium. He dares to go off and bounce into space." Appropriately, "Mork"'s producers hired Winters to play Mork's son when they were trying to revive the show in 1981. That left Pam Dawber with two lunatic aliens to cope with. The result: "We just threw away the scripts and waited to see what happened."

UNCHAINED COMEDY

Robin Williams was probably the only sitcom star ever allowed to make up his own dialogue. "I didn't know whether it would work—improvised television," he said in 1978. "I didn't know whether it would play on screen, whether the cameras could catch it. At first I would go off—from the script—and come back. Now I go off so completely, it's like a happening." The show's writers, tired of seeing their lines thrown out, began tailoring scripts specifically for Williams. They left whole sections blank, with the notation, "Mork can go off here."

RETREAD

Mork's space helmet was actually a prop left over from an episode of "The Outer Limits."

A STAR IS HATCHED

Producer Garry Marshall asked Ronny Hallin, his casting director, to find a comedian to play an alien from the planet Ork. She, in turn, asked Harvey Lembeck, proprietor of a comedy workshop, for the name of the "hottest comic" he knew. Lembeck picked Robin Williams. When Hallin brought Williams in to meet Marshall, Robin was wearing "a pair of glasses made of two soupspoons, each adorned with a white feather." Hallin asked her boss what he thought. "I think," came the reply, "that he's probably from Ork."

SPECIAL EFFECTS

Near the beginning, "Mork's" producers decided against watering down the comedy with special effects. "We did some gimmick things at first," said Robin Williams, "like drinking water through my finger, but we didn't want to go that way with Mork. The gimmicks, the technical tricks, things growing out of your head—that was 'My Favorite Martian.' "

Mork's first appearance was on Garry Marshall's hit sitcom "Happy Days" in 1977. "My ... children had seen Star Wars about five times," says Marshall (above), "and they pestered me about doing a space thing. 'What kind of space thing?' I said. They said, 'Have somebody from the planet Ork.' " So he agreed to do it. It was supposed to be a one-shot performance, but Mork received so much fan mail that ABC decided to give him his own series.

CRITICS' COMMENTS

ABOUT ROBIN:

"Robin Williams is a complete genius; his mind is science fiction all by itself—forget the show. It's like an interplanetary mind."

—**Rick Du Brow,**
Los Angeles Herald Examiner

"Robin Williams would be terrific reading the phone book."
—**Tom Jicha,**
Miami News

"The genius of the show was that it allowed Robin Williams to play Mork in his own way—as a comic. And comics are the aliens who walk among us."
—**Michael Hill,**
Baltimore Evening Sun

"As Mork's character became more sophisticated the show lost some of its comic edge. But even towards the end, it had more bite than most of its competition. In retrospect, there's no news like 'Na-noos.' "
—**Barry Garron,**
Kansas City Star

ON MORK AND GORE:

" 'Mork' was similar to a Gore Vidal play called *Visit to a Small Planet*, which became a Jerry Lewis flick in 1960. Same basic premise—a zany alien comes to Earth and develops a

Exidor (above) believed he could communicate with other planets, but Mork really could. "That wonderful moral at the end, when Mork reports to Orson and tells him the interesting things he's observed about the people of Earth ... accomplishes one of those things that I love about science fiction—it gives us a way of reflecting on ourselves. And getting that alien point of view is something that is valuable to us as a society."

—Warren Norwood, *SF Writer*

close friendship with a woman who introduces him to the baffling nuances of [our] society."
—**Michael Dougan,**
San Francisco Examiner

"If a newborn infant could speak, and give expression to its wonder, he would be Mork."
—**Noel Holston,**
Minneapolis Star and Tribune

"Mork was believable because the value system of his civilization was fairly well explained. During those debriefing ses-

sions with Orson at the end of each show, for instance, you would find out that his planet had a more humane, gentler outlook on life than ours does."
—**Susan Paynter,**
Seattle Post-Intelligencer

THE WILD, WILD WEST

"The Wild, Wild West" became a science fiction show by accident. Michael Garrison, the program's creator, was intent on cashing in on the James Bond craze when he came up with the "retro" angle that placed a macho secret agent named James West in post-Civil War America. "I'm in this for the money," he admitted in 1965. "So we just combined some trends—the Western trend … and the spy [drama]."

But by combining the two genres, he inadvertantly created a third, which captured the futuristic flavor of Jules Verne's novels. It was no longer a Western; gunslingers and cattle thieves had no significance in a world threatened by nuclear weapons. And it wasn't a standard spy show, because the Cold War political tensions that underscored the adventures of James Bond and Napoleon Solo were irrelevant a hundred years in the past. It was a pure science fiction fantasy, based on the tongue-in-cheek speculation that in early Victorian times, mad scientists could have secretly mastered modern technology. James West's foes used computer dating, submarines, torpedoes, ultrasonic sound, and robots in their quest for world domination.

This aspect of the show was handled remarkably well. The villains, played by actors like Victor Buono, Elizabeth Montgomery, Robert Duvall, and of course, Michael Dunn, were convincingly loony. And while the heroes seemed to accept even the most bizarre superscience (in one episode, Miguelito Loveless figured out how to hide in another dimension—inside oil paintings), they never claimed to understand it. The perpetrators were just "evil geniuses," and as everyone knows, there's no limit to what *they* can do. There was also an attractive style in the show. Its technology may have been contemporary, but the design sensibilities were appropriately Victorian. Robots, for example, were steam-powered; and most of the inventions were baroque in appearance.

It probably would have been too one-sided to give the bad guys all of the scientific know-how. So Arte-

mus Gordon, James West's sidekick, did a little inventing of his own; no superweapons—just handy items like explosive buttons and pocket smoke bombs. Gordon also functioned as the show's window into the future, occasionally speculating about flying machines, or psychology. West, the down-to-earth hero who was clearly in awe of his partner's knowledge, would inevitably shake his head in disbelief.

The "The Wild, Wild West" was well acted, and the props (particularly the secret agents' train) were sufficiently convincing. But ultimately, the show was successful because it had a secret weapon: not the time-travel device that one villain invented to alter the results of the Civil War; not the tidal wave machine with which Victor Buono tried to blackmail the United States government; not even the LSD that Miguelito Loveless threatened to drop into the nation's water supply. It was a self-conscious sense of humor. "The Wild, Wild West" worked because even in character, the actors seemed to know that their dilemnas were outrageously farfetched. And yet for an hour every week, they—like their audience—had fun pretending it all made sense.

"This kid will be a big star," the show's producer proclaimed about Robert Conrad in 1967. "He has what Alan Ladd had, only more so. He's fearless, daring—he embodies the fantasies of every boy's dreams."

FLASHBACK

[West has secretly been taken to a crook's hideout in a horse-drawn hearse. Artemus Gordon arrives to rescue him.]

WEST: "Artie! How did *you* get here?"
GORDON: "By hearse—same way you did. Only *I* had to do the driving."
WEST: "How did you know where to come?"
GORDON: "I didn't. The horses did. I just let them go."
WEST: "Ah, that's very clever."
GORDON [with a shrug]: "It's just a practical application of a theory I have about conditioned response. You know, I've got to write a paper about that one of these days."

[West and Gordon are trapped in an old well, and are trying to lower the bucket by tossing stones up into it.]
GORDON: "You know, this might make an interesting game, Bucket Ball."
WEST: "Naw. It'll never catch on."

VITAL STATS

POLL RESULTS:
• Eighth, 627 pts.
PROGRAM INFO:
• Hour show. CBS
• First show: Sept. 17, 1965
• Last show: Sept. 7, 1970
• 104 episodes

BACKGROUND: The press and the public didn't know it, but America was actually in jeopardy almost continuously during the 1870s. A veritable army of criminal geniuses threatened the nation with atomic bombs, robots, submarines, rockets, etc. Fortunately, President Grant found two secret agents who could handle evil scientists quietly and efficiently—James T. West and Artemus Gordon.

West and Gordon are President Grant's personal bodyguards. He provides them with a private train, which they use as a mobile base of operations in their fight against superscientific crime in the sparsely populated Western United States.

THE TRAIN: West and Gordon's headquarters is a plush, private three-car train that includes a kitchen, parlor, bedroom, laboratory, and horse stalls. Weapons and gadgets are strategically hidden throughout: A statue is really a pistol; eggs in the pigeon loft are disguised bombs; pool cues are rifles; billiard balls are smoke bombs; the fireplace is an escape hatch.

HEROES:
• **James T. West** (Robert Conrad): Swashbuckler; pint-sized macho-man. Cool, unemotional, self-assured. An expert shot, master of karate, and proficient in several Samurai techniques. Wears embarrassingly tight pants. Born July 2, 1842.
• **Artemus Gordon** (Ross Martin): Capable fighter, glib liar. Uses disguises to do reconnaisance work and to rescue West. Also an inventor and scientific genius.

VILLAINS:
• **Miguelito Loveless** (Michael Dunn): A dwarf whose ancestors owned much of California during the Spanish occupation. He is determined to get revenge against: 1) the United States for depriving him of his heritage; 2) all of the people who feel superior to him because they're taller than he is; 3) James West, for thwarting his efforts to get revenge on the other two. A brilliant scientist, he invents robots, LSD, cars, electric lights, and even time-travel devices.
• **Count Carlos Mario Vincenzo Robespierre Manzeppi** (Victor Buono): A master magician.

A rare look up at Miguelito Loveless and his partners in crime. Miguelito means "Little Michael;" appropriately enough, actor Michael Dunn, a dwarf, was only three feet six inches tall.

LITTLE BIG MAN

- Miguelito Loveless, played by Michael Dunn, was the best mad scientist TV has ever produced.
- Loveless' inventions were remarkable. As Richard Tharp notes in *Reruns* magazine, "He once stated that he had used mold to concoct a medicine that could wipe out many diseases, perfected a carriage that moved under its own power, and invented a flying machine and a device that transmitted voices over great distances. At ... times, Loveless found ways to alter time and space, and even found a way to shrink living beings without harming them." In fact, after being captured in his first appearance on the series, Loveless insisted on taking a glass bulb with him to prison. He said the device was part of a larger system of sending images through the air, and that he wanted to experiment with it.

- Dunn, a fine actor, was nominated for both Tony and Oscar awards. But he was a troubled man; he committed suicide in 1973.

MISCELLANY

- "The Wild, Wild West" shared its sets with "The Big Valley," another successful Western series of the '60s.
- "The WWW" was a training ground for sf producers. Its two first-season producers, Gene L. Coon and Fred Freiberger, later went on to perform the task on "Star Trek."

MR. MAKEUP

- Ross Martin actually turned down the role of Artemus Gordon five times before finally accepting it.
- He was a real-life "master of disguises"; in almost every

"Dunn loved the role so much that he really came to think he was Loveless."
—Robert Conrad

episode he appeared as at least two—and sometimes three or four—different characters (over one hundred in all). And he did all the makeup himself.
- His characters included: a madam, Robert E. Lee, a Chinese coolie, an 80-year-old minister, an Indian woman, a Hawaiian prince, a Portuguese fisherman, and a magician.
- His fans included Robert Conrad, who once said, "The show worked because it had Mr. Ross Martin, one of the finest actors working today."

Ross Martin was a dedicated trouper. He once broke his leg while filming an episode of "WWW," had a cast put on, and kept on filming. The producers shot him from the waist up so the cast wasn't visible.

CRITICS' COMMENTS

ABOUT ITS APPEAL:

"It worked because it was an unlikely blending of the familiar and unfamiliar—that totally bizarre juxtaposition of a cowboy riding to save the world from a nuclear explosion."

—**Robert Jordan,**
SF Writer

"What made the show work wasn't *one* character, but the combination of both West and Gordon. They were a balanced team—West was an athletic, swashbuckling type; Gordon was more cerebral, the one who operated by his wits. They were inseparable as friends, and inseparable as heroes. The show depended on both of them."

—**Robert Laurence,**
San Diego Union

"Ross Martin made the show. James West was the *central* character, but Artemis was the *unique* character. [He] became the vehicle for all the imagination in the program."

—**Greg Bailey,**
Nashville Banner

ABOUT ITS SUPERVILLAINS:

"Miguelito Loveless ... I mean, my God, in nineteenth-century America? This crazed master genius had it all over Professor Moriarty—there was just something so wonderful about that. If you had a fantastical image of reality at all, you always felt, as

"The villains were always bigger and badder than life, but Conrad played a straight character—and within limitations even Ross Martin was straight—which enabled him to transmit the feeling that, yeah, they really could be in jeopardy from some of these evil schemes."

—R.K. Shull, *Indianapolis News*

you were growing up, that this kind of thing really happened somewhere, but you were never going to *know* about it. In 'The Wild, Wild West,' you get to *watch* it."

—**Peter Pautz,** *SF Writer*

ON WWW AS SF:

"The concept behind 'The Wild, Wild West'—an alternate past—was original for television. They speculated a great deal of high-tech, evil scientists, and other science fictional elements happening in the Old West. Yet ... they actually made it possible for viewers to suspend disbelief for awhile and accept that somewhere, sometime, this could've happened in America—that there might've been a government agent run-

ning around in the 1870s, trying to put down evil scientists from a train car."

—**D. Douglas Fratz,**
THRUST—The Magazine of Science Fiction

"The 'Wild Wild West' is sort of science fiction in retrospect. The contraptions and inventions were late Victorian, but the show was set [much earlier]. ... It was a novel idea, going back into the past and writing a far-future science. Of course, it was completely off the wall; we know that—but if you were sitting in your drawing room in the Victorian era, this is what you might have viewed as science fiction possiblities."

—**C.J. Cherryh,**
SF Writer

V (The Miniseries)

Out of the hundred-plus science fiction series that have aired nationally since 1950, only a handful have fulfilled science fiction's higher purpose of addressing social or political issues—and most of *them* were largely ignored by viewers.

So "V," the miniseries, was a rarity: a science fiction drama with a serious political statement *and* a huge prime time audience.

On the surface, it was simply another tale of alien invaders (in this case, horrible lizard creatures disguised as human beings) who were trying to take over our planet. But in "V," it was the aliens' *methods* that counted. They didn't ravage Earth, they ruled it. They wooed collaborators by offering them positions of power. They used propaganda to portray themselves as society's saviors ("The Visitors Are Our Friends"). And then they ruthlessly herded their enemies into concentration camps. The Visitors were, in fact, space Nazis. They even sported an insignia resembling the swastika.

That was the crux of "V." The inspiration for the program wasn't a love of science fiction; it was producer Richard Johnson's apprehension about right-wing activity in America. "I'm concerned about fascism in the United States," he explained in 1983. "There's a great complacency in this country and nothing seems to shake us. What if the Fascists started herding us off in box cars?"

Fascists in America isn't a subject guaranteed to attract good ratings—even in the Reagan era. But Johnson was determined to get his point across. After toying with the idea of portraying an invasion by foreign troops—maybe Russians or Chinese—and deciding the public would never accept the premise (he was ahead of his time; ABC did it in 1987 with "Amerika"), he settled on presenting his ideas as pure science fiction fantasy—an alien takeover. And sure enough, the public loved it. Each miniseries was among the highest-rated programs of the year.

Johnson's creation had the benefit of good writing, modern special effects, and the largest budget in TV history (at the time). It also had fine perfor-

Andrew Prine, the head of the Visitors' security.

mances from Mark Singer and Faye Grant as the resistance leaders, Andrew Prine as the the head of security, and best of all, Jane Badler as the Visitors' terrifying leader ("a sort of female Dr. Mengele," one critic called her). But it is the clearly stated political metaphor that makes "V" memorable.

Typically, network executives didn't understand this. Seduced by the miniseries' ratings, NBC hungrily adapted "V" into a weekly series in 1984—without Johnson's blessing or participation. They converted "V" into a pointless alien versus human shoot-'em-up, and drove the Visitors off the planet for good after only one season.

Jane Badler was one of the miniseries' main strengths, simultaneously alluring and repulsive as Diana.

FLASHBACK

DONOVAN [looking at the preserved humans in the deep-freeze room]: "Why are they being taken … stored like this? Why not just killed?"

MARTIN: "The Leader needs them living. Some of them will be made into troops for battle with his enemies. …"

DONOVAN: "What about the others?"

MARTIN: "In addition to the water … there is another … basic shortage on our planet."

DONOVAN [suddenly understanding]: "—*Food* !"

DIANA [addressing other Visitors]: "The problem is that our Leader says, 'Why not convert them all?' He doesn't understand that the human will is much, much tougher than we bargained for. To convert them all would take forever."

VITAL STATS

POLL RESULTS:
• Ninth, 576 pts.
PROGRAM INFO:
• Two four-hour miniseries. NBC
• First show: May 1-2, 1983
• Second show: May 4,5,6, 1984

BACKGROUND: In the late twentieth century, a fleet of spaceships arrives on Earth, carrying humanoids from an unnamed planet. They proclaim friendship and offer advanced technology in exchange for the right to extract certain minerals. Earth agrees. The Visitors slowly take control of our planet, using a campaign of terror and propaganda. In truth, they aren't benevolent at all—nor are they really humanoids. They are carnivorous lizard creatures (cleverly disguised) whose world was depleted of its basic resources. Secretly they steal Earth's water and refrigerate humans for future meals. Not everyone accepts this new staus quo. A resistance movement springs up, and with the aid of a fifth column of Visitors who disapprove of the mission, they attempt to drive the aliens away forever.

MAIN HEROES:
•**Mike Donovan** (Marc Singer): A TV news reporter who managed to get aboard a mother ship and learn the truth about the Visitors. Independent, a man of action. He works with the resistance.
•**Dr. Julie Parris** (Faye Grant): A scientist who escapes the Visitors' concentration camp (set up to eliminate scientists who could penetrate their disguises) and becomes leader of the underground. Efficient, compassionate, strong-willed.
•**Ham Tyler** (Michael Ironside): Soldier of fortune, the resistance movement's technical expert.
• **Robin Maxwell** (Blair Tefkin): A naive teenager who gives birth to the first interspecies baby.

• **Elizabeth** (Jennifer Cooke): Interspecies "star child" born to Robin; outwardly human, with tremendous mental powers she can't yet control.
•**Willie** (Robert Englund): A gentle pro-human Visitor.

MAIN VILLAIN:
•**Diana** (Jane Badler): Officially in charge of the science section of the Visitors, but the de facto leader of the expedition. Killed John, the original leader, when he began losing control. Arrogant, ambitious, with a voracious appetite for food (live mice), sex (even with humans, although that seems disgusting to other V's), and power. Voted by critics as their favorite science fiction TV villain ever.

For a while, "V" was an international fad; a great deal of collectible merchandise was produced. A package of Portuguese trading cards.

3 20$00

Colecção de 81 Calendários

A BATALHA FINAL

Cost Conscious

The budget for the first "V" miniseries was $13 million—$3.3 million per televised hour—the most expensive made-for-TV production ever. But it was immediately topped by the *second* miniseries, which cost *$14 million*. What did they spend it on? Sample expenses:
- 6,500 uniforms were used in the two miniseries.
- The aliens' "conversion chamber" cost $250,000 to build.
- A six-second shot of "a small spaceship diving toward Earth" cost $25,000.
- Each blast from a laser rifle cost the studio $1,000.

Inspiration

Believe it or not, the idea for calling his show "V" came to

Kenneth Johnson in a men's room.

"I was in a men's room washing my hands, looking at the grafitti on the wall one day while I was writing the script, and it brought to mind that in all the research I was doing on World War II, I kept seeing grafitti written on the walls in London. And the principal graffiti during the war was 'V' for victory. … I had this image of a British woman with a Doughboy helmet on, wearing a housedress, huddled behind a pile of rubble with a rifle in her hand. And nearby was a wall with a V painted on it. … It occurred to me that that was the right title, because that was what the picture was all about."

Food, Glorious Food

- By far, the most popular special effect in the miniseries was the Visitors' mouse-eating trick.

It looked so real that some people gagged just watching it.
- It was accomplished by giving the actor a false throat with a built-in set of air sacs that inflated and deflated in sequence, so it looked as though the mouse was sliding down his/her throat.
- When the alien leader (Jane Badler) ate a rodent on screen, she was really downing a chocolate mouse, something she *did* object to in real life—not because of the concept, but because of the calorie content.

Creator's Comments

"The first script that I wrote had nothing to do with science fiction. It was a very realistic piece. It was suggested that I put it into a science fiction vernacular, using aliens as the Nazis. I wasn't thrilled by it at first, because I was tired of doing that sort of thing. But then I realized it was the proper way to go."

The cast of "V" poses for a science fiction magazine. (Photo © Movie Publishers' Distributors)

CRITICS' COMMENTS

Kenneth Johnson, "V" 's creator

ABOUT IT'S PREMISE:
"Kenneth Johnson came up with some really interesting, introspective things about human behavior. The same way that Gene Roddenberry used science fiction to talk about how human beings are, how we behave, etc., in 'Star Trek,' Johnson used it in 'V' to talk about our whole attitude toward freedom and the subtle ways you can lose it."

—**Gary Gerani**,
Fantastic Television

ON ITS POLITICS:
"When I saw 'V,' I immediately thought of *It Can't Happen Here*, by Sinclair Lewis, because it drew the same parallels to fascism in America. In both, the enemy seemed benign—but had ulterior motives and its own agenda. And the general populace was sort of apathetic about what was going on as they lost their freedom little by little. In a kind of mass, comic-book

style, 'V' brought out the same points that the novel did."

—**Duane Dudek**,
Milwaukee Sentinel

" 'V' is the only show *ever* in which heroes and heroines are part of a leftist underground. It's a political statement, made during a very conservative era. ... Unlike the movie *Red Dawn*, it's not the Communists who are attacking the United States, but aliens from outer space who represent Nazi Germany. So the heroes are part of a guerrilla war against fascists, and they *know* it. ... I found that fact very interesting."

—**Danny Peary**,
Cult Movies

ON THE UNIFORMS:
"It's an old idea, but it gave the science fiction convention-goers who like to dress up an easy one to copy—those red and gold uniforms were very popular right away, as you might have guessed they'd be."
—**Fritz Leiber, SF Writer**

ABOUT SPECIAL EFFECTS:
"The outer-space shots, with the spaceship, etc. are all very well done in a standard sort of way. ... But the best science fiction comes when you put an unexpected twist on something very common—and 'V' 's special effects were really used well in that way. The two most striking scenes in the program were a woman giving birth and a woman eating. No big deal, right? Except that one woman gave birth to a *half-lizard*, and the other one ate a *mouse*. That was pretty frightening. In fact,

the mouse scene was so well done that I just said, 'That's all for me.' "

—**Michael Berlyn**,
SF Writer

ABOUT THE QUESTIONS IT RAISES:
" 'V' is 'Amerika' with lizards—suddenly we're all under the domination of an outside force. ... And if you can accept that premise, then you have to wonder: How would you react? Would you be a collaborator? Would you be in the resistance? Or would you just mind your own business?"

—**Tom Jicha**,
Miami News

"In most TV science fiction, networks seem to feel they've got a better chance to succeed if they keep things bland. And yet looking at 'V' 's success, you have to wonder if they aren't outsmarting themselves."

—**Jack Mingo**,
The Couch Potato Handbook

"'V' lacked the basis in sound scientific principles which is a requirement of all good science fiction. For example: The universe is full of water—why did the Visitors come here, where they'd have to fight for it? And when you consider all the possible routes evolution can take, the probability of aliens having humanoid forms—albeit with scaly skin—is basically zilch. On top of all that, the notion that these intergalactic lizards and earthlings would be genetically compatible is too absurd to even contemplate."

—**Michael Dougan**,
San Francisco Examiner

THE PRISONER

Patrick McGoohan wouldn't have included "The Prisoner" in this volume. "This is a contemporary subject," he said in 1967, "not science fiction. [And] I hope that will be recognized by the audience." But genre classification is in the eye of the beholder, and critics made McGoohan's bizarre allegory the strongest write-in choice on this list.

"The Prisoner" is more like a Kafkaesque fantasy than a standard science fiction program. A fiercely independent man awakens to find himself confined in a little village. Where is it? No one will tell him. Why is he there? No one will tell him. Who is in charge? No one will tell him. He spends the entire series struggling with—and trying to escape from—the authorities, who are intent on wiping out his sense of individuality.

Although everything in "The Prisoner" is clearly symbolic, it's *not* clear exactly what things are symbolic *of.* McGoohan leaves his audience as much in the dark as the Prisoner seems to be, and critics are free to draw their own conclusions.

"You might call this 'New Wave science fiction,'" said one, "because it deals with the condition of man, and what man *could* do in certain situations. It asks questions about the condition of man—'Are we free?' and 'What exactly is society? What is it doing to us? What can we do to it?' New Wave science fiction deals with social issues more than with technology." Another added, "I think that science fiction is about alternate realities, alternate possiblities. And in that context, 'The Prisoner' is a speculation about the condition of what it is to be alive more than a scientific extrapolation."

Clearly, "The Prisoner" is also television's interpretation of a dystopia, or anti-utopia; a stepchild of George Orwell's *1984.* Orwell's 1949 novel examined the ways in which technology could—and, implicitly, *would*—be used to undermine individual freedom in the near future. It postulated a society monitored by two-way TV screens ("Big Brother Is Watching You"), rendered intellectually impotent

Patrick McGoohan says that not even he knew that the Prisoner would turn out to be Number 1 until the series was almost over. "It got very close to the last episode, and I hadn't written it yet, and I had to sit down--this terrible day--and write the last episode." After the episode was aired, McGoohan had to go into hiding to avoid irate fans. (Photo courtesy ITC Entertainment, Inc.)

by self-canceling cliches and slogans ("War Is Peace"), and brainwashed into conformity with sophisticated mind-control techniques.

Seventeen years later, Patrick McGoohan picked up that thread of speculation and wove it into a conventional TV format. The world is not as bleak in "The Prisoner," nor is it as large—most of the action is confined to a small oceanside community. But Big Brother is still watching (there are electronic eyes everywhere), and science is clearly used to break the human spirit. Everyone dresses alike, thinks alike, speaks alike. Democracy is a sham. And the only man who treasures his independence—Number 6—is isolated, an enemy of the state.

McGoohan never purported to be speculating on the future, however. In his eyes, Orwell's nightmare has already begun. "The Village is our little world," he once told a reporter. "Big Brother is here."

Number 6 in the Village. (Photos courtesy ITC Entertainment, Inc.)

FLASHBACK

NUMBER 6: "Has it ever occurred to you that you're just as much a prisoner as I am?"

NUMBER 2: "Oh, my dear chap, of course! I know too much. We're both lifers. I am definitely an optimist. That's why it doesn't matter *who* Number 1 is. It doesn't matter which side runs the Village."

NUMBER 6: "It's run by one side or the other."

NUMBER 2: "Oh, certainly. But both sides are becoming identical. What in fact has been created is an international community—a perfect blueprint for world order. When sides facing each other suddenly realize that they're looking into a mirror, they will see that *this* is the pattern for the future."

NUMBER 6: "The whole world as the village?"

NUMBER 2: "That is my hope. What's yours?"

NUMBER 6: "I'd like to be the first man on the moon."

VITAL STATS

POLL RESULTS:
- Tenth, 554 pts.
- Write-in

PROGRAM INFO:
- Hour show. CBS
- First show: June 1, 1968
- Last show: Sept. 11, 1969
- 17 episodes

TIME: Tomorrow.

PLACE: The Village, a mysterious community surrounded by "The Mountains" and "The Sea." No one seems to know where it is or who runs it. Populated by docile ex-intelligence operatives and a few women in mod outfits.

BACKGROUND: The Prisoner resigned his job as a secret agent. But as he packed his belongings, preparing to go on vacation, he was gassed and kidnapped. He awoke in the Village, where he was told he was now called Number 6. Various authority figures—each calling himself Number 2—attempt to break him and learn why he resigned, but Number 6's will is too strong; he won't give in. His time is spent plotting escapes and trying to discover the identity of Number 1.

HERO: Number 6 (Patrick McGoohan): English citizen; never named. Born March 19, 1928, at 4:31 A.M. Joined the air force during World War II, but was shot down and spent time as a POW. After the war, became an intelligence agent. A man of steely determination and almost inhuman self-control; brilliantly analytical, widely read, an Olympic fencer and boxer. Favorite pastime (apart from planning escapes): koshu, a sport played on trampolines.

OTHER: The Butler (Angelo Muscat): Number 2's manservant, a dwarf who never speaks, smiles, or shows any emotion.

VILLAINS:
- **Number 2** (various actors/actresses): Strong-willed, clever, erudite. The only visible sign of the ruling force of the Village, since Number 1 is never seen. He/she has total power over the community, but failure of any sort results in

removal and replacement. Number 6 has broken several Number 2's. They change regularly.
- **Rover**: The final line of defense for the Village. A semi-lifelike creation, a huge white rolling ball that is programmed to capture or kill potential escapees. Can be launched from the monitor room. Has limited sentient capability.

Just a pawn in their game. The idea for "The Prisoner" originally came from script editor George Markstein, who suggested a drama about the escape attempts of an imprisoned secret agent. Markstein envisioned a standard spy show, but McGoohan used the theme to express his own ideas about life. Toward the end of the series, Markstein quit because he wanted the Prisoner to get away, and McGoohan refused to let him escape. (Photos courtesy ITC Entertainment, Inc.)

THE VILLAGE

The Village is actually on the grounds of the Hotel Portmeirion, at Penrhyndeudraeth in North Wales. It was built by Sir Clough Williams-Ellis, a noted architect, over several decades. McGoohan first discovered it when he went there to film some episodes of "Secret Agent" several years earlier. "I thought it was an extraordinary place, architecturally and atmospherically," McGoohan explains, "and should be used for something." So "The Prisoner" was actually created to make use of the setting. Trustees of the resort agreed to let McGoohan use it for the show, but only if he promised not to reveal the location until the last episode. They

explained that didn't want to be overrun with fans.

EFFECTS

Actor/executive producer Patrick McGoohan relied on the atmosphere of Portmeirion rather than special effects to give life in the Village an other-worldly quality. The only elaborate special effect he planned was Rover—and that failed: McGoohan's SFX crew built him a machine "like a hovercraft," which could go anywhere—under water, up walls, along the beach, etc. But on the first day of shooting, the machine broke down; it went into the water and never came back up.

McGoohan was in trouble; without a Rover, he couldn't film the show. But as he stood

"Freedom is a myth."
—Patrick McGoohan

staring at the place where his machine had sunk forever, a weather balloon drifted by. "How many of those can you get me?" he asked his assistant. The assistant rushed off in an ambulance to find out, and returned with one hundred of them. They became the new Rover— now transformed from a high-tech machine into a killer balloon.

NUMBER 6?

• Most people assume that Number 6 is John Drake, the secret agent from McGoohan's previous hit series, "Danger Man" (or "Secret Agent"). He's not, although he's intentionally similar. "John Drake … is gone," McGoohan announced in 1967, "but we're not foolish enough to change the image we've established with TV audiences."

• It's also a common myth that in the last episode, Number 2 says, "I'll see you later, Drake." The real line is, "I'll see you after a coffee break."

• Even if he'd wanted to, McGoohan couldn't have used the name "John Drake;" it was owned by "Danger Man's" creator, Ralph Smart.

• To emphasize the difference between Number 6 and Drake, all biographical details released about Number 6 were actually McGoohan's (e.g., both McGoohan and Number 6 were born on 3/19/28).

" 'The Prisoner' captured its time perfectly—it took the restlessness of that decade, the late '60s, and turned its distaste for authority into a work of art."
—Ed Siegel, *Boston Globe*

CRITICS' COMMENTS

ABOUT THE HERO:

"It wasn't important to the nature of the show that that character be explored in any normal way. He became a symbol of man fighting for personal freedom, and like all such symbols, he wasn't a real person. ... He was kind of a superman—a man with unshakeable principle and the determination to escape."

—**Gary Gerani,**
Fantastic Television

ABOUT THE EFFECTS:

"The best special effect was that big, white rolling ball that kept people on the island from escaping. It looked like a giant wad of Playdoh, but it was still threatening. The way people kept getting squished and absorbed by it was just sufficiently icky looking to make you say, 'Ecch, what a way to go ... slimed to death.' "

—**Bob Wisehart,**
Sacramento Bee

ON ITS FORMAT:

"I like any show that gives you a minimum of information and allows you to make up your own show as you go. 'The Prisoner' was...the Colorforms of TV."

—**Joel Pisetzner,**
Bergen Record

" 'The Prisoner' didn't explain a lot. ... It was a completely bizarre environment, a thoroughly bizarre situation, and you knew there were no answers— you knew you were never going to find out about it. But there was something compelling about the continuing mystery of the show."

—**Pat Murphy,**
SF Writer

ABOUT PRISON:

"Before I'd ever heard of 'The Prisoner,' I was invited to a lecture given by a psychiatry professor at Columbia Univerisity. His interpretation ... was that the entire thing is a psychotic fantasy—that there's no such place as the Village, that the Prisoner hasn't been kidnapped...that this is a paranoid-schizophrenic delusion. ... The implication, of course, is that the character is being imprisoned in his own mind, and nowhere else. ... [McGoohan] is basically saying that there is no such thing as freedom, because you're always imprisoned by your own psychological state."

—**George Alec Effinger,**
SF Writer

THE INVADERS

In the early '50s, science fiction movies rooted in the political paranoia of McCarthyism appeared at drive-ins all over the country. They were referred to as "They're Here" films, because the theme of each was an insidious takeover by aliens who looked and acted like normal Americans; like the Commies (as many people believed at the time), the aliens' strategy was infiltration and subversion from within. The style reached its apex in 1956 with *Invasion of the Body Snatchers*, and as America emerged from the shadow of the Cold War, "B" moviemakers found other ways to exploit our latent fears.

Ten years later, the genre was resurrected for television in "The Invaders." But there were no political implications this time around; the perpetrators just liked the idea of scaring the pants off their audience. Or as producer Alan Armer declared in 1967: "We're selling paranoia."

The premise of "The Invaders" was unique for TV: A man knew that aliens were scheming to take over our planet, but he had to convince people he wasn't crazy (and keep from going crazy himself) before he could save the world. And if that wasn't already tough enough, it seemed that the only "people" who took him seriously—the ones he learned to love and trust—frequently turned out to be Invaders themselves. In the best episodes, he could never be sure who was really on his side until the end of the show. "The reason ['The Invaders'] is terrifying," explained Armer, "is that it's done with real people, and everyone is suspect. ... It's not a whodunit, but a who is it—which are actually the aliens?"

It *was* scary, but in retrospect, "The Invaders" may have been too ambitious an undertaking for a regular series. Its message was communicated through the star's internal torment—his frustration, fear, isolation. Episodic TV, however, depends on action, and the show inevitably became repetitious as the hero, David Vincent, crossed the country week after week crying, "The aliens are coming" to an unbelieving public. In fact, many critics dismissed it as just another "running man" series because it was masterminded by Quinn Martin, the producer responsible for "The Fugitive."

However, there were real gems among the forty-nine episodes. One tense drama featured a trial for murder in which the accused claimed his victim had been an alien; Vincent couldn't tell if it was legitimate or if he was being played for a fool. Another, called "The Mutation," had Vincent barely eluding an alien plot to eliminate him because the Invaders' agent, played by Suzanne Pleshette, was a mutant with human emotions (the Invaders normally had none). Her sympathy for his plight cost her life; and the anguished hero retaliated with a rifle, picking off a bunch of the literally heartless aliens. But what good did it do him? There were always more.

"The Invaders" lasted only a year and a half. Yet it's fair to say that the producers achieved their goal. Critics *still* remember being frightened by it; the show is gone, but after two decades, the paranoia remains.

VITAL STATS

"In order to remain in human form, the aliens have to regenerate themselves every 10–12 days, and we have bizarre, kookie machinery for this purpose," explained the show's producer just before it premiered in 1967. "The machinery is clearly not of our civilization or technology."

POLL RESULTS:
• Eleventh, 572 pts.
PROGRAM INFO:
• Hour show. ABC
• First show: Jan. 10, 1967
• Last show: Sept. 17, 1968
• 43 episodes

TIME: Now (actually the late '60s).

PLACE: The United States.

BACKGROUND: Architect David Vincent, too tired to keep driving, parks in a secluded spot to sleep for a while—and is awakened by a landing flying saucer. A bad dream? Authorities think so; Vincent knows better—the fate of Earth rests in his hands. He begins a one-man crusade to stop the Invaders, who need a new home because their own planet can no longer support life. The aliens' plan: take over Earth's institutions from within the system, a little at a time. Prognosis for Vincent's battle: hopeless.

HEROES:
• **David Vincent** (Roy Thinnes): The monomaniacal foe of the Invaders. An architect by training, he has one married sister and no other ties. Despite the scorn and ridicule he attracts with his tale of UFOs, he makes himself a public figure to whom the helpless can turn for aid against the Invaders. He will answer any call, investigate any story, go anywhere in his quest.
• **Edgar Scoville** (Kent Smith): Millionaire businessman (electronics) who learned the truth of Vincent's claims firsthand. Heads a small group of people known as "The Believers," who back Vincent up when he needs assistance; they finance the unending war against the Invaders.

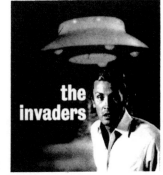

the invaders

VILLAINS:
• **The Invaders**: Survivors of a dying world who appear human but are actually amorphous beings needing periodic recharging (in "regeneration chambers") to retain their disguises. Without regeneration, they revert to natural form and perish in Earth's deadly atmosphere. Can assume any shape, but the imitation is never perfect. The most obvious mark of an Invader: It can't bend its little fingers. Invaders do not possess human emotions (and thus seem cold and aloof), or have heartbeats. When they're killed, they disintegrate in a red glow, leaving only a few ashes and a burnt outline. Their science is more advanced than ours; they have interstellar crafts and ray-guns, but their most potent weapon is a small disc which is applied to the back of a victim's neck. It produces death of apparent heart failure.

FLASHBACK

NARRATOR: "The Invaders … alien beings from a dying planet. Their destination: the Earth. Their purpose: to make it their world. David Vincent has seen them. For him it began one lost night on a lonely country road, looking for a shortcut that he never found. It began with a closed, deserted diner and a man too long without sleep to continue his journey. It began with the landing of a craft from another galaxy. Now David Vincent knows that the Invaders are here, that they have taken human form. Somehow he must convince a disbelieving world that the nightmare has already begun."

TRUE GRIT

It's amazing that David Vincent didn't spend most of his time at the dentist; it seemed as though he spent the entire series gritting his teeth. The more frustrating the situation, the harder you'll see him clench his jaw.

CLEVER EFFECTS

"In the planning stage," says executive producer Quinn Martin, "it was decided to use special effects as little as possible. Theme, character, and plot were more important." Yet the effects were a significant element of the show. A few simple tricks made them more striking:
•**Color:** Taking advantage of America's increased use of color TVs, they made the aliens' flying saucer more interesting by drenching it in colored lights.
•**Design:** "The interior of the spaceship, ray-guns, and energy-charging tubes were made to look like things not too far in the future," Martin says, "so people could relate to what was happening."
• **Restraint:** The aliens were actually shown in their natural form on the series only once— and the image was intentionally blurred so viewer wouldn't be able to make out any details. The producers felt it was better to leave the Invaders' real appearance to the audience's imaginations. They also never revealed the name or location of the Invaders' home planet.

HAND JIVE

In the series, David Vincent could identify most Invaders by their crooked pinkies. But that wasn't the original concept. Initially, the plan was to give the aliens a disappearing *eye* in the middle of each palm. ABC rejected it.

THE VISIONARY

Roy Thinnes claimed to have seen a UFO while he was working on "The Invaders." Did it make *him* paranoid, too? Not in the slightest. He traveled around the country encouraging a dialogue about friendly aliens. "The character I played and I shared the same futility," he said years later, "—the inability to convince authorities that visitors from other galaxies were not necessarily as aggressive as we are, that they could bring peace and health to our ... planet."

"I don't think Thinnes (left) would have been my choice," Larry Cohen, creator of "The Invaders" once admitted. "I was looking for someone with a little more vulnerability than he displayed."

Roy Thinnes and William Windom in an episode of "The Invaders."

CRITICS' COMMENTS

ABOUT THE PREMISE:
"The paranoids are after us!"
—**Andy Porter,**
Science Fiction Chronicle

"The possibility that it *could* be real made it good science fiction. As a kid … it made me paranoid, and I thoroughly enjoyed that."
—**Jeffery Fuerst,**
TV Historian

"Who is real, and who isn't? The evidence always disappeared—the aliens' bodies went up in a little blaze of light when they were dead—so the main character could never say, 'I've killed an alien; here's his body.' He knew the truth, but he couldn't prove it and nobody believed him. That paranoid element adds an extra dimension."
—**F. Paul Wilson,**
SF Writer

ABOUT THE MAIN CHARACTER:
"Roy Thinnes reminded me a lot of David Janssen in 'The Fugitive.' He had the same sort of attitude—that kind of quiet, sweaty desperation—and he always seemed to be grinding his teeth. Think of how frustrated he must have been. Nobody would listen to him—or if anybody did, they died by the end of the show. … Yet he kept plowing ahead; in a way, I found that really heroic."
—**Bob Wisehart,**
Sacramento Bee

"Thinnes had no sense of humor. His character was just totally determined, totally monomaniacal, and as a result, not particularly interesting—which is where the series faltered, because the aliens wound up being more interesting than the humans on the show."
—**Jack Mingo,**
The Couch Potato Handbook

ABOUT THE STORIES:
"What could David Vincent do? If he proved the aliens were there, the series was going to end. So it had to be the same thing every week: He finds the aliens somewhere; he tries to convince people of it; they don't believe him; they find out; it's too late; the aliens get away somehow. Considering how difficult a premise it was to work with, they managed to pull it off pretty well."
—**Harry Castleman**,
Watching TV

"One of the reasons 'The Invaders' wasn't successful was its utter sense of hopelessness; I mean, these aliens were winning. In every episode David Vincent would be close to accomplishing something, and in every episode the Invaders would stop him. … I think it was one of the most depressing shows that's ever been on TV; he got his clock cleaned every week."
—Steve Sonsky, *Miami Herald*

QUARK

Adam Quark, garbage collector in outer space. (Photo courtesy Columbia Pictures)

Historically, neither satire nor science fiction has been very popular with large TV audiences. So you can imagine how well a show that combined *both* of these genres would fare; "Quark," television's first adult science fiction parody, lasted for two months and exactly eight episodes in 1978.

Critically, however, this amusing and original work was well-received. "This is funny stuff," observed *TV Guide* in its April 1, 1978, issue; "Richard Benjamin may be the perfect spoof hero." And *Variety* added: "Benjamin has...a flair for comedy, so the project [is] off to a good start. Sci-fi fans should settle in and enjoy the outrageousness."

Unfortunately, *only* sf buffs enjoyed it; the rest of the country was tuned in to "Wonder Woman" and "Donny and Marie." As a result, "Quark" remains a little-known cult show today. It's the science fiction community's secret, a joke seemingly invented especially for them.

In a way, this makes sense; to really appreciate the program's humor, you have to be familiar with the details of the genre. For example, practically every stock sf TV character is lampooned in the spaceship's crew. The usual high-tech robot companion, called Andy (for android) in "Quark," is no help at all—he's an undiscriminating heap of junk that falls in love with a load box in the pilot episode; the requisite macho space fighter and helpless female are combined into one genetic mutant that can't make up its mind whether to fight or fawn; there's a clone and a clonee aboard, each of whom claims to be the original human; and the head of operations—usually no more than an offscreen voice—is a disembodied head. Meanwhile Adam Quark, the dashing space captain, is just a bumbling schnook. There's a Spock send-up, too—a logical plant named Ficus who expresses contempt for his emotional companions. Of course, his logical conclusions are often wrong, but then, that's logical, too.

And the plots are takeoffs of specific films or TV programs. The opening episode is a *Star Wars* parody featuring a blundering cosmic power called "The Source" (Quark: "Don't use it to clean portholes—save it for the biggies, like good versus evil"). In another adventure, a spoof of a "Star Trek" episode called "The Deadly Years," Quark 's presence is requested by a beautiful princess; but he passes through a strange gas and by the time he arrives, he has aged so much he can barely move.

Unfortunately, there are too few episodes to expect "Quark"'s return in reruns. But perhaps someday soon Columbia Pictures will release the program on video and make it possible for people who missed "Quark" the first time around to see why critics named it one of the best science fiction shows of all time in this poll.

The Barnstable twins—Cyb and Trish—were the Doublemint twins before they made their TV series debut in 1978 as a lovable airhead and her clone.

FLASHBACK

In "The Source," a Star Wars parody episode, Quark has been following the advice of a disembodied voice called the Source (voice supplied by Hans Conreid)—which keeps getting him into trouble.

THE SOURCE: "*Trust me.*"

QUARK: "Why should I trust you? You're always wrong!"

SOURCE: "Because … I am … the Source!"

QUARK: "The source of *what*? I can't see … I'm standing on this light bridge … there's a thing down there that wants to eat my head. I don't think I need any more of your help."

SOURCE: "You quitter!"

VITAL STATS

POLL RESULTS:
• Twelfth, 480 pts.
PROGRAM INFO:
• Hour show. NBC
• First show: Feb. 24, 1978
• Last show: April 14, 1978
• 8 episodes

BACKGROUND: By the year 2222 A.D., man had mastered space travel and was moving freely around the galaxy. But wherever there's life—even in outer space—there are piles of trash. So the United Galaxy Sanitation Patrol was established. Its headquarters: Perma One, a huge space station run by the Head (literally, just that). Its mission: to go where all men have gone before, and clean up the garbage they've left behind. Capt. Adam Quark and his crew must fly around picking up weightless baggies of garbage which other spacecraft have ejected. Tools of the trade: Quark's ship is outfitted with mechanical hands called Waldoes.

QUARK AND CREW:
• **Adam Quark** (Richard Benjamin): Well-meaning but incompetent. An unintentional buffoon who dreams of more romantic assignments than trash-collecting.
• **Gene/Jean** (Tim Thomerson): A transmute, born with a full set of both male and female chromosomes. Result: has a male *and* a female personality. They switch at unpredictable times, flipping him from macho Gene to shy, retiring Jean. Particularly troublesome in combat situations.
• **Ficus** (Richard Kelton): An ambulatory plant know as a Vegeton. Must be watered frequently. Totally unemotional, devoted to logic; chooses the worst possible moments to ask questions. Has sex by lying on his back and waiting for a passing bee to pollinate him.
• **Betty I and Betty II** (Tricia and Cyb Barnstable): Semi-clothed, sexy airheads. One is human, the other a clone—but no one knows which is which. They speak and act in unison.
• **Andy the Robot** (Bobby Porter): Faithful robot companion. Childish and cowardly android with limited capabilities; he's built out of spare parts and looks like it.

Conrad Janis played Palindrome.

AND: Otto Bob Palindrome (Conrad Janis): A resident of Perma One, Quark's pedantic, fussy, nervous boss. Contemptuous of Quark and terrified of his own boss, the Head. Has panic attacks whenever Quark is on a mission—usually *because* Quark is on a mission.

ACCIDENTAL PART

•Richard Benjamin's role in "Quark" was a coincidence. He'd worked with "Quark" creator Buck Henry before—Henry had written the script for *Catch 22*, in which Benjamin starred—but Henry had never considered contacting him for the TV series because he was known as a film actor.

•Benjamin, who normally never read *Variety* magazine, happened to flip through it in his dentist's office one day in 1977; he noticed a report that Henry was writing a pilot script for a comedy called "Quark."

•"Science has always fascinated me," he explained in 1978, "so I knew what a quark was, and if Buck was writing it, I felt it could only be a satire on the outer-space movies, the sort of spoof Buck did on the spy movies with 'Get Smart.' " On a whim, he called Henry—and got the lead role.

SPACED OUT

The pilot for "Quark " was filmed in early 1977, months before the *Star Wars* phenomenon made science fiction an "in" topic. It aired in May 1977 and received good ratings—so it seemed a sure bet for NBC's fall schedule. But it was passed over. Buck Henry personally visited the actors who'd starred in it and gave them the bad news.

But when the *Star Wars* craze swept America, NBC took another look—and commissioned

The Head, real boss of Perma One. (Photo courtesy Columbia Pictures)

"It was pretty silly, but it was also full of wild, inventive comedy."
—Richard Benjamin

eight episodes of the series. In terms of ratings, however, NBC was right the first time. Hardly anyone watched the show during its brief run, and no more "Quarks" were ever made.

WHAT'S IN A NAME?

For the layman, Buck Henry explained why he chose the title of the show: "In scientific lingo, a quark is the smallest part of the nucleus of the atom. Adam Quark is the smallest, the last part of the intergalactic space patrol—yeah, the name is fitting."

"Quark"'s creator, Buck Henry. By the time the show reached the air, Henry was no longer in charge of it. And his absence may have meant the difference between survival and cancellation. As *TV Guide* put it: "Buck Henry, a known loony who contributed to 'Candy' and other comic assaults, created the series. If he stays around to keep it funny, space opera may never recover." Rumor has it that he was relieved of command because he and NBC disagreed on how much should be spent on the show's sets.

CRITICS' COMMENTS

ABOUT THE STAR:

"Benjamin is one of the greatest comedic actors ever. In 'Quark' he was like Alex Reiger [of 'Taxi']. ... Except he wasn't in a taxi dispatch station—he was in outer space looking for empty beer cans, looking for Hefty bags around Saturn. The idea was so bizarre that I loved it."

—**Ken Hoffman,**
Houston Post

"Benjamin wasn't the most memorable character in it—but then, he never is. He was the average schmoe, surrounded by craziness."

—**Dusty Saunders,**
Rocky Mountain News

"Benjamin's a middle-class TV husband stuck in space. Like Fred Flintstone, or Riley, or even Archie Bunker out there on the spaceways, with the kind of job Archie Bunker might actually have."

—**Michael Cassutt,**
SF/ TV Writer

ABOUT ITS HUMOR:

"'Quark' is really a perfect parody miniseries, because each episode was set up as a straight send-up of a particular aspect of popular science fiction. One was their *2001* parody; another was a *Flash Gordon* takeoff; another was a 'Star Trek' parody;

and the pilot was a *Star Wars* satire. When you realize that, each individual episode becomes hilarious."

—**Walter Podrazik,**
Watching TV

"I like the idea of an intergalactic garbage man being the star of a series. I would like the idea of any *garbage man* being the star of a series—just to make it somebody who isn't a cop or a detective. But 'Quark' didn't do strange enough things—it wasn't that much funnier or more outrageous than some of the *unintentionally* bad science fiction on TV at the time."

—**David Bianculli,**
New York Post

ABOUT WHY IT FAILED:

"I thought it was ahead of its time. In fact, if it were to come on today, it still might be ahead of its time."

—**Bob Wisehart,**
Sacramento Bee

"The problem ... is that television is a mass medium, and the larger the mass, the harder it is to be individual. ... A show like 'Quark' would've had to be much dumber and broader—and it was plenty broad anyway—to succeed."

—**Robert Silverberg,**
SF Writer

"One of the fundamental problems with a show like 'Quark' is that it's a satire, and before you can satirize something, you've got to actually see it done right. There's never been a science fiction show on TV that you could say has been 'done right.' So 'Quark' was doomed before it started."

—**Jeffrey Carver,**
SF Writer

(Photo courtesy Columbia Pictures)

The Jetsons © 1987, Hanna-Barbera Productions

THE JETSONS

"The Jetsons" isn't often mentioned in conjunction with science fiction; certainly William Hanna and Joseph Barbera had other things in mind when they unveiled the series in 1962. Two years earlier "The Flintstones" had debuted on ABC as the first network prime time cartoon show in TV history and was an immediate smash. (It remains the only animated series ever to rank in the Neilsen annual Top 20). Trying to duplicate their success, Hanna-Barbera studios simply inverted the "Flintstone" formula; instead of transposing contemporary American society into the prehistoric past, they projected it into the future. The result was a space-age sitcom with none of the philosphical tension (good versus evil, humanity versus technology, etc.) associated with most classic science fiction. It was all strictly for laughs.

But that was the point. "The Jetsons" was a reassuring fantasy about everyday life in a safe and familiar future; science fiction for a young population living in a decade of mind-boggling change.

To appreciate "The Jetsons," you have to view it in context. When it debuted in September 1962, the space race was beginning in earnest. John Glenn, the first American astronaut to circle the Earth, was our national hero; NASA had publicly declared its intentions to put a man on the moon by the end of the decade; space-age products like freeze-dried food and pocket calculators were starting to appear. America was excited by the future—but we were also scared of it. At President Kennedy's urging in 1961, homeowners built fallout shelters en masse. And a month after the first episode of "The Jetsons" aired, the world came dramatically close to nuclear war with the Cuban Missle Crisis.

So George and Jane Jetson's arrival, in their cute atomic space vehicle, was a welcome one. Up there in the Skypad Apartments, they had the future fantasy life we all dreamed of. They could have anything they wanted, just by pushing a button; they had a robot to do the housework (no more "Clean up your room before you go out to play"); they even had a telephone with a screen attached, so you could actually *see* the person you were talking to. Even the toys were neat: Elroy's little rocket ship was just what we wanted for Christmas.

The Jetsons' future is a soothing vision of happy middle-class people and friendly machines. And because it has been shown in reruns almost continuously for the last twenty-five years, it has had more impact on today's adults than many serious sf programs. Scratch a baby boomer, and you'll find that his or her secret fantasies of life in the future include a few of the Jetsons' great gadgets ... and an uneasy feeling that he or she might just wind up working for Cosmo Spacely at Spacely Sprockets some day.

Mr. Spacely gives George Jetson a piece of his mind. In the 21st century, people work three hours a day, but that's still too much for George. The Jetsons, © 1987 Hanna-Barbera Productions, Inc.

FLASHBACK

What do you remember about the Jetsons? Can you come up with:

1. The name of Elroy's and Judy's schools?
2. What George did for a living?
3. Rosie the Robot's nickname for Elroy?
4. How the Jetsons got Rosie?
5. Astro's original name?
6. Mr. Spacely's first name?
7. The name of Spacely Sprockets' biggest rival?

ANSWERS:

1. The Little Dipper School; Orbit High.
2. He was an Automated Index Operator at Spacely Space Sprockets.
3. Roy-Boy.
4. She was obsolete and all they could afford.
5. Tralfax Gotrocket.
6. Cosmo.
7. Cogswell's Cosmic Cogs.

VITAL STATS

POLL RESULTS:
• Thirteenth, 465 pts.
PROGRAM INFO:
• Half-hour cartoon. Originally, ABC.
• First show: Sept. 23, 1962
• Last show: Sept. 8, 1963
• 24 original episodes

TIME: Late in the 21st century.

PLACE: Orbit City.

BACKGROUND: For middle Americans like the Jetsons, family life hasn't changed much since 1962. Approaching the year 3000, Dad (George) is still the reluctant breadwinner and head of the household; Mom (Jane) still handles the domestic chores; the kids (Elroy and Judy) still like rock 'n' roll and hate school—which they're still forced to attend every day.

The only thing that's really changed is the way technology pervades their everyday lives. Their home in the Skypad Apartments, for example, has a built-in hydraulic lift that elevates them above the clouds in inclement weather; they travel around the city in a nuclear-powered airmobile; when it's dinnertime, they turn to the "foodarackacycle," a push-button machine that instantly delivers any food they select; doctors make house calls through a video screen that descends from their ceiling; their maid is a robot named Rosie.

Of course, new technology brings new problems. In one episode, Jane nearly has a nervous breakdown because she has too many buttons to push. But the big stuff we worried about in the twentieth century doesn't seem to be a bother any more. There's no pollution, no over-population, and the ozone layer is still intact.

THE FAMILY:

• **George** (voice: George O'Hanlon): A slightly harried, harmless 35-year-old cross between Fred Flintstone and Ward Cleaver .

• **Jane** (voice: Penny Singleton): A wife and mother with an addiction to shopping. Always attired in the latest space-age fashions.

• **Judy** (voice: Janet Waldo): A cool 15-year-old chick with a punk ponytail. Loves boys, parties, and dancing.

• **Elroy** (voice: Daws Butler): A 9-year-old electronics whiz who's probably smarter than his father. Wears a space-age beanie.

• **Rosie the Robot Maid** (voice: Jean Van der Pyl): Always ready with a sarcastic comment or a broom and dustpan.

• **Astro** (voice: Don Messick):The overeager, slobbering family pooch. Scooby Doo's forerunner.

The Jetsons, © 1987 Hanna-Barbera Productions, Inc.

Rosie the robot maid. The Jetsons, © 1987 Hanna-Barbera Productions, Inc.

FUTURE STOCK

"The Jetsons" introduced some of the most interesting high-tech labor-saving devices ever displayed on the small screen. Their futuristic household gadgets included:
•A solar-powered stamp licker.
•A seeing-eye vacuum cleaner that hunted up dirt on its own (and swept it under the rug when Mrs. Jetson wasn't looking).
•A voice-operated washing machine that washed, dried, and folded clothes in thirty seconds.
•A nuclear-powered knitting machine.
•A dog-walking treadmill that came complete with its own fire hydrant.

They didn't have everything, though. As George once remarked, "After a century of brilliant scientific progress, you'd think someone would invent a decent flyswatter."

WHOSE VOICE

Chances are, you've heard the Jetsons' voices before.
•George O'Hanlon played William Bendix's neighbor in "Life With Riley."
•Penny Singleton played Blondie in the '40s movie series.
•Daws Butler is the voice of Yogi Bear and Cap'n Crunch.
•Janet Waldo played Penelope Pitstop.
•Don Messick is Scooby Doo and Dr. Quest in "Jonny Quest."

Elroy gets set to head down the pneumatic tube to the Little Dipper School. The Jetsons, © 1987 Hanna-Barbera Productions, Inc.

•Jean Van der Pyl is Wilma Flintstone.
•And Mr. Spacely's voice belongs to that "wascal" Mel Blanc.

MISCELLANY

•"The Jetsons" was the first program ever televised in color on ABC-TV.

"Meet George Jetson. ... His boy Elroy ..."

•It was a prime-time flop, but a weekend success. After its 1962 debut, the show aired for fifteen consecutive years on Saturday morning—on all three networks. It's an amazing record when you realize there were only twenty-four episodes to recycle.
•It took sixteen months and 1,600 sketches to come up with George Jetson—the same amount of time it took to create the entire rest of the family.
•In 1985, Hanna-Barbera created new "Jetsons" episodes and resyndicated the series.

Below: Jane chats with George over the videophone. Strangely enough, when "The Jetsons" first aired, Bell Telephone was experimenting with this invention. They predicted that by the end of the '60s, everyone would be using it, and introduced it commercially in 1965. It didn't go over because of the expense. Rates for the first three minutes from N.Y. to Chicago, for example, were $13.50. The Jetsons, © 1987 Hanna-Barbera Productions, Inc.

CRITICS' COMMENTS

ABOUT THE CHARACTERS:

" 'The Jetsons' was reverse 'Flintstones,' but it was better than 'The Flintstones.' The characters were more fun, George Jetson being much more likable than Fred Flintstone (albeit much more of a nebbish). They were both supposed to be sort of satires on modern life, but the Jetsons worked better because it's funnier to see a modern setting extrapolated into the future than it is to see one thrust into the past."

—**Harry Castleman,**
Watching TV

"Unfortunately, the future, if we have one, is going to be boring, not adventurous; more suburban than the New Frontier. George Jetson is a role model for the future of man and humanity, where the biggest excitement will be choosing synthetic breakfasts."

—**Jack Mingo,**
The Couch Potato Handbook

ABOUT THE JETSONS' FUTURE:

"Maybe, by making us laugh at the future a little bit, 'The Jetsons' made us a little less afraid of the future."

—**Mark Dawidziak,**
Akron Beacon-Journal

ABOUT JETSON TECHNOLOGY:

"The people who created 'The Jetsons' were probably familiar with the 1939 World's Fair. ... I remember that my mother used to say 'The Jetsons' reminded her of things she'd seen at the New York World's Fair. The futuristic notions that were introduced there worked their way into the popular consciousness, and 'The Jetsons' really drew on that."

—**Pat Cadigan,** *SF Writer*

" 'The Jetsons' appealed to me because it said, no matter how advanced the technology gets, things aren't going to change much. It was as if the Flintstones were thrust into the future without missing a beat. Oddly, some of the visions of 'The Jetsons'—like moving sidewalks—have actually come to pass."

— **Barry Garron,**
Kansas City Star

"My favorite [science fiction special effects] were in the Jetson household; especially the bed that turns into a toaster and pops George out of bed in the morning. Been waiting for that one to come on the market for years!"

—**Debbi Snook,**
Cleveland Plain-Dealer

"Science and technology in the Jetsons' world is like magic in the classic fairy tales. Pushbuttons just take the place of magic wands. It's 'Poof!' and you've got a meal."

—**Melissa Schwarz,**
Harmony Books

The Jetsons, © 1987 Hanna-Barbera Productions, Inc.
"I loved it when the Jetson family sat down for a meal at the Foodarackacycle, their push-button cook."
—Ron McCutchan, *Science Fictioneer*

CAPTAIN VIDEO

"Captain Video" was TV's maiden voyage into the cosmos—the first sf TV show. Taking a cue from the popular space serials of radio and film (e.g., *Flash Gordon* and *Buck Rogers*), the tiny DuMont network launched its new program over the airwaves in 1949. "Captain Video! Master of Science! Guardian of the Universe!" it proclaimed. The live serial quickly became the rage for kids, and was actually one of the shows responsible for helping to sell TV sets in the medium's early years.

Despite its popularity, however, you could hardly call "Captain Video" a great show; in fact, by today's standards it was ludicrous. It was like watching grown-ups play "spaceman" with cardboard boxes and discarded hardware. Even in 1950, the actors had to work at containing their laughter. "We have to run through it to get the laughs out," admitted the original Captain Video, Richard Coogan. "The lines are so corny that we always break up in rehearsal. If it was all new when we got on camera, we couldn't keep a straight face."

In 1951, a reviewer for *The New Yorker* magazine tried describing an episode: "The scene shifted to a coldly forbidding room, the decor of which I assumed, based on my science fiction reading, to be other-planetary. ... Two men in the room were wearing odd-looking uniforms, which were not quite military and not quite [non-]military. One of them had epaulets the size and shape of water-wings, and he kept inquiring, 'Did you get to the airport?' The other fellow, a garrulous type, made no sense at all. Another uniformed man, hitherto in the shadows, stepped forth, pulled a knife from his shirt, and smirked. When he had wiped the first smirk off his face, he smirked a second time, without difficulty."

Obviously, adults couldn't fathom the show's attraction. But "Captain Video" was never aimed at adults. It was a vehicle for childrens' imaginations.

Captain Video and the Ranger, America's first TV astronauts.

To kids, it didn't matter that the Captain wore a doctored-up US Army outfit or that the weapons in his comic-book arsenal looked suspiciously like ordinary household objects. They were in awe of the power of science, and captivated by the possiblities. We already had the atom bomb, and rockets, and even television itself. Why not space travel? Why not Opticon Scillometers? Why not Cosmic Vibrators? So as they watched Captain Video, a whole generation of American children were propelled into the space age. Many of today's critics were among them, and they paid homage to the Captain by including his show on their list of TV's best science fiction programs.

Richard Coogan played the Captain for one year, then left in 1950 to star in a Broadway play with Mae West.

FLASHBACK

EVERETT [speaking into headphones]: "Chauncey Everett here, aboard the *Polar Star*, calling Captain Video, aboard the *Galaxy*. ... Microwave channel Delta one-two-three, Gamma three-six-nine. Do you read me, Captain?"

CAPTAIN VIDEO: "Jumpin' Saturnian salamanders! Now what?"

CAPTAIN VIDEO: "Out here in the black void of space there are millions of people on these planets who hunger for a word from home—just a letter from loved ones they may have left on planet Earth. That's why the Ranger and I have fought to prove that an interplanetary mail system can be used."

VITAL STATS

POLL RESULTS:
• Fourteenth, 410 pts.
PROGRAM INFO:
• Fifteen-minute, half-hour shows. DuMont network
• First show: June 27, 1949
• Last show: 1956 (syndicated)

BACKGROUND: In 2254 A.D. Captain Video—the greatest scientist in history—set up a secret mountain fortress and became the "Guardian of the Safety of the World." His mission: to protect Earth from evil.

Assisting him on Earth were a legion of Video Rangers, many of whom patrolled the Old West on horseback (actually old cowboy films, inserted to save production expense), and later a youngster known only as the Ranger. Although he had no super-powers, the Captain's arsenal of superweapons made him almost invincible. Among them: the Remote Tele-Carrier, which enabled him to see anything anywhere in the world on a television screen; the Opticon Scillometer, which allowed him to see through walls; the Astra-Viewer, an incredibly powerful telescope that enabled him to observe life on distant stars; and the Cosmic Vibrator, a ray-gun that shook his opponents into submission.

HEROES:
• **Captain Video** (Richard Coogan, 1949–50/Al Hodge, 1951–55): An all-American who hated evil, but rarely killed anyone (he preferred to shake them). Jet pilot, moral paragon, inventor extraordinaire, and a space ace who patrolled the universe in his spaceship, the *Galaxy*.
• **The Ranger** (Don Hastings): The Captain's 15-year-old sidekick, "The idol of every young television fan in America."

Al Hodge takes the Captain Video Pledge on "The Merv Griffin Show" in 1975.

MAIN VILLAINS:
• **Dr. Pauli** (Hal Conklin): Head of the Asteroidal Society, an evil scientist as brilliant as Captain Video, and thus his arch-enemy. Inventor of the Cloak of Invisbilty, the Trisonic Compensator (which made bullets turn corners), and the Barrier of Silence (allowed him to move noiselessly). He was killed four times, and was brought back each time by popular demand.
• **I Tobor**: Voice-activated giant indestructible robot (robot = Tobor spelled backwards) who fell into the hands of the evil Atar. Fought the Captain to a standstill (Tobor's powers were as great as Video's) until the Captain disguised his voice to sound like Atar's. Confused, Tobor short-circuited. He, too, was brought back by popular demand.

" 'Captain Video' 's influence is not limited to its round-eyed televiewers. Last month Fawcett Publications put the captain between the covers of a comic book. Last week Columbia Pictures announced the filming of a fifteen-episode movie serial based on the Captain's adventures. 'I guess we've arrived,' says [the show's creator] proudly."

—*Time* magazine, Dec. 25, 1950

LIVE AID

Cutting financial corners in live TV sometimes created absurd and embarrassing situations. In *The Great Television Heroes*, Donald Glut and Jim Harmon tell this story: "Once, the [minuscule] budget was exhausted before two necessary props—a doctor's bag and a stethoscope—could be purchased [for an episode]. Minutes before the show went on the air, the crew realized that they didn't have the props. Two employees dashed to a department store, one returning with a toy stethoscope, the other with a full-size suitcase.

"Not only the performers, but the entire crew exploded into laughter [on national TV] as the actor playing the doctor opened the suitcase, which contained nothing but the tiny stethoscope, and tried in vain to make the instrument reach both ears."

EFFECTS

"Captain Video" had the lowest special effects budget of any major TV show in history—only $25 a week—which, even in 1950, didn't go far. For example:
• The *Galaxy*'s control panel was just a painted board. The rest of the ship's interior was made of cardboard.
• Pilots wore leather football helmets and business suits in space.

• The Captain's snappy uniform was actually World War II military surplus.

CAPTAIN NICE

Al "Captain Video" Hodge was a good guy off screen, too. He taught Sunday school on weekends, and believed he was performing a worthwhile function with his TV show. "At least three times a week on 'Captain Video,' " he said, "we deliver short messages to our youthful listeners. We stress the Golden Rule, tolerance, honesty, and personal integrity. I'm thankful for the opportunity to be associated with a show that helps, in a small measure, to illuminate for the young people of America the importance of courage, character and a sense of moral values."

Despite the fact that he'd once been the idol of millions of American children, Al Hodge was unable to get work as an actor after his show folded in 1956. But after living in obscurity for over a decade, Hodge was rediscovered in the late '70s. He had just announced his comeback when he was found dead in a New York hotel in 1979.

CRITICS' COMMENTS

ABOUT THE EFFECTS:

"The special effects were pretty tacky, but when you're a kid, you don't require much to prick your imagination. So it seemed perfectly adequate—even lavish—to us at the time. "

—**Tom Shales,**
Washington Post

"They didn't have much to work with. To simulate space travel, they'd put a [toy] spaceship on a wire, put a sparkler on the end of it, and throw it. … And sometimes the thing didn't even make it all the way off the screen.

"In the back, through the porthole, they had this starscape that was a continuous loop. They would just keep rolling it by, so the same constellations would go past, time after time after time.

"But as a kid, I wasn't bothered that the special effects were so blatantly bad because I knew that they couldn't really get into outer space to take those pictures. … We just used our imaginations and … filled in the things they did with [visions] of what it might really be like."

—**Warren Norwood,**
SF Writer

ABOUT FANTASY:

"The wonderful thing about 'Captain Video' was that it had radio writers [creating the scripts]. They were so good at concocting tight little formats that you were drawn into the show's momentum, even though you knew the actors were standing behind a kitchen sink with a couple of doo-dads on it, not a spaceship control panel. When the guy shook the camera, and Captain Video would look out and see whatever was out there, your imagination clicked right in."

—**David Jones,**
Columbus Dispatch

ABOUT ITS WRITERS:

"I was surprised to discover, years later, that many science fiction writers who were my early heroes—Jack Vance, Damon Knight, and [a few others]—wrote for 'Captain Video.' A lot of guys who were having trouble paying the rent, paid the rent by writing 'Captian Video' [episodes]. … They were paid a hundred dollars a week to turn out that stuff."

—**Robert Silverberg,**
SF Writer

" 'Captain Video' showed a child the possibility of space exploration—of where science could take you ... the sense of wonder about what is possible for us as human beings to accomplish, to get off the planet and explore other worlds and not admit to any earthbound limitations."

—**F. Paul Wilson,** *SF Writer*

THE ADVENTURES OF SUPERMAN

"The Adventures of Superman" was syndicated by Kellogg's cereal beginning in 1953, fifteen years after the Man of Steel first appeared in *Action Comics #1*. It was a milestone science fiction show. The hero, for example, was the first alien being to be featured as a main character in a weekly TV series—although, as one critic noted, "He was so convincing as a fighter for 'truth, justice, and the American way' that we usually forgot he was from another planet altogether."

"Superman" also stands out as the prototype superhero program—the father of shows like "The Hulk," and "The Greatest American Hero." But it accomplished a great deal with very little. The average episode cost only $15,000 to complete, and each was shot in an assembly-line fashion. Lois, Clark, and Jimmy, it turns out, always wore the same suits of clothes during the program's run because scenes from several different episodes were filmed simultaneously. The producers thought it was too expensive to invest in wardrobe changes every time they switched stories.

"Superman"'s most important contribution might be as a TV pioneer in filmed special effects. Live shows like "Space Patrol" and "Tom Corbett" did the best they could, but only "Superman" was visually convincing in the early years of television. It didn't take much imagination to believe in the Man of Steel when you could actually *see* him soar through the skies over Metropolis, smother bombs with his chest, and smile as he smashed through brick walls. Of course, by today's standards, the effects were often laughable. In the debut episode, the enemies were midgets with plastic caps over the tops of their heads; their superweapon was an Electrolux vacuum cleaner. And the iron bars George Reeves "bent with his bare hands" were obviously made of rubber. But in the unsophisticated '50s, the effects were exciting. They enabled us to believe in the magic of Superman—the Space Messiah who arrived on planet Earth to save us from ourselves.

"Superman" was ahead of its time in another way: it featured a regular troupe of characters who, like the cast of "Taxi" and "Mary Tyler Moore" in later years, functioned as a family in the workplace—each with a predictable personality, a defined role, and a standard vocabulary of one or two phrases (like "Great Ceasar's ghost!" and "Jeepers, Mr. Kent!").

One of them still talks about the experience: "The biggest memory I have of playing Jimmy Olsen," recalls Jack Larsen, "is that I was always tied to a chair with a bomb at my feet ... and George would break through the walls to rescue us. [I'd always say,] 'Golly Superman, I thought you were never going to get here.' " He didn't mean it, of course; Superman always got there. That was one of the few things we could count on at the beginning of the atomic age.

George Reeves poses with Phyllis Coates, the first Lois Lane. After "Superman"'s successful debut season, Coates was offered an opportunity to star in a TV pilot. She took the chance—which gave Noel Neill her "big break" on TV. P.S.: Coates's pilot never became a series.

FLASHBACK

Lois Lane [mooning over Superman]: "Clark, does spring mean anything to you?"
Clark Kent: "Baseball."
Lois [sheepishly]: "Do you think spring means anything to Superman?"
Clark: "He doesn't have time for baseball!"

Clark, playing poker with some crooked gamblers, uses his X-ray vision to ignite the cards.
Lois: "That deck seemed to just explode in flames."
Clark: "Maybe it was a hot deck."

Lois: "Superman and you ... I still wonder. ..."
Clark: "Wonder? It's no wonder you wonder. You're a pretty wonderful girl."

VITAL STATS

POLL RESULTS:
•Fifteenth, 383 pts.
•Write-in
PROGRAM INFO:
•Half-hour show. Sydicated
•First show: 1953
•Last show: 1957
•104 episodes

TIME: The 1950s (present-day when the series was made).

LOCATION: Metropolis, a major American city.

BACKGROUND: Jor-El, a leading scientist on the planet Krypton, discovers that his world is doomed. After trying unsuccessfully to convince Krypton's rulers to construct huge spaceships and evacuate the entire population, he begins building a rocket large enough only for his own family. But before he can complete it, Krypton self-destructs; there is only enough time for Jor-El and Lara to save their infant son, Kal-El, by shooting him into space in a tiny test rocket.

Kal-El eventually crash-lands in a field outside of Smallville, USA. There he's discovered by a childless farm couple named Martha and Jonathan Kent, who adopt him and name him Clark. As the mild-mannered youngster grows, he discovers that because he's from a larger world with a red sun, he has miraculous powers on Earth: super-strength, superhearing, X-ray vision, flight, and a host of other abilities. He becomes known as Superboy, fighting crime and injustice, but keeps his identity secret so criminals can't harm his Earth parents. At age 25, he moves to Metropolis and gets a job as a reporter for *The Daily Planet*. Now he secretly doffs his suit, glasses, and hat and becomes Superman whenever he's needed.

MAIN CAST:
•**Superman** (George Reeves): The ultimate good guy. Likes to break through walls instead of going through doors. His only weaknesses: Kryptonite and bad puns.
•**Clark Kent** (George Reeves): Superman's alter-ego, a meek fellow who doesn't like to make waves.
•**Lois Lane** (Noel Neill): Star reporter for the *Planet*. Has a propensity for taking outrageous risks, and constantly needs to be rescued by Superman. She's madly in love with him, but thinks Clark is a wimp.
•**Jimmy Olsen** (Jack Larson): Cub reporter for the *Planet,* and Superman's pal. Admires Clark and wants to be a great reporter like him.
•**Perry White** (John Hamilton): The *Planet's* crusty editor-with-a-heart-of-gold.
•**Inspector Bill Henderson** (Robert Shane): The Metropolis police officer somehow assigned to all of Superman's cases.

George Reeves surveys the scene in a classic Superman pose. Before Reeves became Superman, the show's producers had tested more than 200 actors for the role. Then Reeves wandered into their office one day; he instantly won the part because, explained the producer, "He looked like Superman with that jaw of his." Reeves's first response: "Superman? What's that?" And later: "I've played about every type of part you can think of. Why not Superman?"

"It's really jolly up there zooming around in my blue longies and red cape."

—George Reeves

illusion of landing from a great height.

• For those shots of Superman flying over Metropolis, Reeves was filmed laying on a glass table; the sky behind and cityscape below him were matted in later.

I.Q. TEST

The supporting characters were played tongue-in-cheek by the cast. "It wasn't camp, but you had to play it light," says Jack Larson. "After all, Jimmy and Lois never figure out that Superman is Clark Kent. They're obviously very dumb people".

BIG BANG

The earliest "Superman" episodes were a little on the violent side. But when Kellogg's (the sponsor) realized that the audience was mostly children, the violence was toned down and the villains just became "humorous bumblers." "Most of the time," said director Whit Ellsworth, "rather than Superman beating up those guys, we'd shoot them running into each other or cracking their heads on the wall." In one episode, Lois and Jimmy actually thwarted a pair of crooks by hitting them in the face with pies.

TV SPORTS

• **NONSEQUITURS:** The show is full of inconsistencies, and fans love to catch them. Like: Crooks will almost always empty their guns at Superman, who stands there bravely with his hands on his hips as bullets bounce off his chest. But when the crooks toss their empty guns at the Man of Steel, he ducks. And: Although Lois is a reporter, she never takes notes.

• **CRIB SHEETS:** John Hamilton, who played Perry White, kept forgetting his lines. So he was always filmed sitting behind a desk littered with papers— among them the script. Try to spot it.

TAKING FLIGHT

The special effects that enabled George Reeves to "fly" weren't sophisticated. At first, a simple system of wires and pulleys lifted him into the air. But after a wire snapped and almost killed him, a counterbalance, powered by a hydraulic unit, was devised. Other effects were even simpler:
• For more exciting takeoffs, Reeves used a springboard. He'd take a little jump, then vault over the camera and onto a tumbler's mat behind it.
• For Superman's dramatic landings, Reeves simply jumped from a stepladder, accompanied by a "whooshing" sound effect that created the

CRITICS' COMMENTS

ABOUT THE CHARACTERS:

"Lois and Jimmy had an engaging simplicity which paralleled television's own simplicity. ... It was a show in its infancy for a medium that was in its infancy, and the characters were child-like as well."

—**Alex McNeil,**
Total Television

"We were all little Jimmy Olsens, watching that show."

—**Gordon Javna, *60s!***

"My favorite character was Inspector Henderson, because he believed in Superman and was willing to turn his police authority over to a guy from another planet. ... I mean, can you imagine a police chief in New York City going on TV and saying, 'We have no power to control this, but maybe the Man of Steel can help'—and then looking at a subway, waiting for Superman to appear?"

—**Ken Hoffman,**
Houston Post

"Superman is the character all little kids wanted to be—including me."

—**Danny Peary,**
Cult Movies

ABOUT SPECIAL EFFECTS:

"Even on a little TV screen, black and white, with cheap special effects, I was caught up in the wonder of the planet Krypton, of Superman's time travels, of Superman splitting in two and having to confront *himself.* "

—**Walter Podrazik,**
Watching TV

"My favorite special effect in all science fiction TV is George Reeves flying, as Superman, with his stomach pressed flat by the invisible table he's laying on. And when he flies right to left, the S is backwards."

—**Michael Uslan,**
TV Producer/Writer

ABOUT HIS MORALS:

"Superman in the TV series strikes me as a real Christian. Here's a man who says what he believes, and then lives that way. I remember one episode in which two criminals steal his costume and try to use their knowledge of his secret identity to blackmail him. It was a moral dilemna that Superman couldn't resolve—he couldn't do all the things that immediately came to mind, like killing them or locking them away forever, because he wouldn't compromise his principles for any reason. How many role models like *that* did we have?"

—**Peter Pautz, *SF Writer***

CLASSIC OPENINGS

Science fiction programs have always had great introductions. Here are a few memorable ones.

"THE ADVENTURES OF SUPERMAN"
(1953-57)
"Look! In the sky!"
"It's a bird!"
"It's a plane!"
"It's Superman!"
"Yes, it's Superman, strange visitor from another planet, who came to Earth with powers and abilities far beyond those of mortal men. Superman, who can change the course of mighty rivers, bend steel in his bare hands; and who, disguised as Clark Kent, mild-mannered reporter for a great Metropolitan newspaper, fights a never-ending battle for truth ... justice ... and the American way!"

"BATTLESTAR GALACTICA"
(1978-79)
PROLOGUE: "There are those who believe that life here began out there, far across the universe, with tribes of humans who may have been the forefathers of the Egyptians, or the Toltecs, or the Mayans. Some believe there may yet be brothers of man who, even now, fight to survive, somewhere beyond the heavens."
EPILOGUE: "Fleeing from the Cylons' tyrrany, the last battlestar, *Galactica*, leads a ragtag fugitive fleet on a lonely quest—for a shining planet known as Earth."

"CAPTAIN VIDEO"
(1949-56)
"Captain Video! Master of space! Hero of science! Captain of the Video Rangers! Operating from his secret mountain headquarters on the planet Earth, Captain Video rallies men of good will everywhere. As he rockets from planet to planet, let us follow the champion of justice, truth, and freedom throughout the universe."

"ROD BROWN OF THE ROCKET RANGERS"
(1955-56)
"CBS television presents ... 'Rod Brown of the Rocket Rangers'! Surging with the power of the atom, gleaming like great silver bullets, the mighty Rocket Rangers' spaceships stand by for blast off! ... Up, up, rockets blazing with white hot fury, the man-made meteors ride through the atmosphere, breaking the gravity barrier, pushing up and out, faster and faster and then...outer space and high adventure for ... the Rocket Rangers!"

"STAR TREK"
(1966-69)
"Space, the final frontier. These are the voyages of the starship *Enterprise*. Its five-year mission: to explore strange new worlds; to seek out life and new civilizations; to boldly go where no man has gone before."

"THE TIME TUNNEL"
(1966-67)
"Two American scientists are lost in the swirling maze of past and future ages during the first experiments on America's greatest and most secret project—the Time Tunnel. Tony Newman and Doug Phillips now tumble helplessly toward a new, fantastic adventure somewhere along the infinite corridors of time!"

CLASSIC OPENINGS

"The Outer Limits."

"TOM CORBETT, SPACE CADET"

(1950-56)

"Space Academy, USA, in the world beyond tomorrow. Here the Space Cadets train for duty on distant planets. In roaring rockets, they blast through the millions of miles from Earth to far-flung stars and brave the dangers of cosmic frontiers, protecting the liberties of the planets, safeguarding the cause of universal peace in the age of the conquest of space!"

"THE TWILIGHT ZONE"

(1959-63)

"There is a fifth dimension beyond that which is known to man. It is a dimension as vast as space and timeless as infinity. It is the middle ground between light and shadow, between science and superstition, and it lies between the pit of man's fears and the summit of his knowledge. This is the dimension of imagination. It is an area which we call the Twilight Zone."

"SPACE PATROL"

(1950-56)

"High adventure in the wild, vast regions of space! Missions of daring in the name of interplanetary justice! Travel into the future with Buzz Corey, commander in chief of ... the Space Patrol!"

"THE OUTER LIMITS"

(1963-65)

"There is nothing wrong with your television set. Do not attempt to adjust the picture. We are controlling transmission. If we wish to make it louder, we will bring up the volume. If we wish to make it softer, we will tune it to a whisper. We will control the horizontal. We will control the vertical. We can roll the image; make it flutter. We can change the focus to a soft blur, or sharpen it to crystal clarity. For the next hour, sit quietly and we will control all you see and hear. We repeat: There is nothing wrong with your television set. You are about to participate in a great adventure. You are about to experience the awe and mystery which reaches from the inner mind to ... the Outer Limits."

"THE PRISONER"

(1967)

"Where am I?"
"In the Village."
"What do you want?"
"Information."
"Whose side are you on?"
"That would be telling. We want information."
"You won't get it!"
"By hook or by crook we will."
"Who are you?"
"The new Number 2."
"Who is Number 1?"
"You are Number 6."
"I am not a number. I am a free man!"

THE SEXIEST ROBOT OF ALL-TIME. In the '60s, TV executives played a game with sitcoms, trying to pander to male sexual fantasies without actually mentioning sex. They put, for example, Gilligan and two other bachelors (Thurston didn't count) on an island with two good-looking women; they had the gorgeous Jeannie ("I Dream of Jeannie") living in sin with her "master"; and then they had this one, "My Living Doll," a fantasy about a bachelor (Robert Cummings) and his gorgeous live-in companion, Rhoda (Julie Newmar). Actually, Rhoda's name was AF 709. She was a robot designed by Dr. Carl Miller, who left her in the care of Army psychiatrist Dr. Robert McDonald while he traveled in Pakistan. What did McDonald do with a robot who looked like Julie Newmar? What would *you* do? Rhoda just obeyed orders.

MOST FAMOUS TV ROBOT: The "Bubble-headed Booby"

from "Lost in Space." He was created by Bob Kinoshita, who designed the sets—including Robby the Robot—for the classic sf film, *Forbidden Planet*. The Robot was no mechanical wonder in real life; an actor (Bob May) was inside the costume hitting a telegraph key whenever he spoke, so that the lights on his chest blinked in time with the dialogue. Movement was accomplished two ways: When viewers could see the whole Robot, he was pulled on wheeled blocks, using hidden wires. When the bottom half of the Robot was obscured in a scene, the actor inside wore what they called "the Bermuda Shorts"—a duplicate Robot suit with the bottom cut off, enabling the actor to walk.

John Schuck, a fine TV actor, somehow wound up playing Yoyo in "Holmes and Yoyo." Yoyo was an experimental robot developed by the police department, assigned to work with Detective Alexander Holmes, because Holmes' partners kept getting injured. The top brass figured they'd give Holmes a partner who couldn't be hurt. The result: three months of goofy sitcom antics, then cancellation.

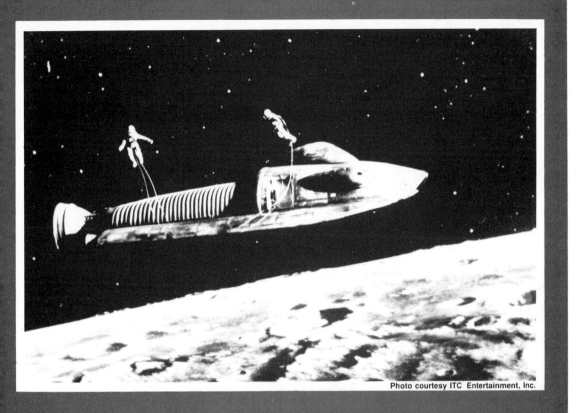

Photo courtesy ITC Entertainment, Inc.

The Critics' Choice:
The 10 Worst Science Fiction TV Shows of all Time

SPACE: 1999

The parts of Koenig and and Russell were originally written for Robert Culp and Katherine Ross—who turned them down. So Martin Landau and Barbara Bain got them by default. The hour-long show was syndicated in both the 1976 and 1977 seasons, but after forty-seven episodes, production ceased. (Photo courtesy ITC Entertainment, Inc.)

This selection is no surprise to science fiction fans who tuned in the show in 1976 anticipating a new "Star Trek" and found a disappointing collage of wooden characters, boring dialogue, and incomprehensible plots instead. As Cleveland Amory wrote in *TV Guide* at the time, "This series wasn't produced—it was committed, like a crime."

The acting was inexplicably bad. With the main characters played by "Mission: Impossible"'s popular husband/wife team, Barbara Bain and Martin Landau, it was reasonable to expect at least a competent job. But in "Space: 1999," these two accomplished performers were pathetic. Landau, as the head of the moon colony, was grim and emotionless. Bain was so stiff that critics compared her to a zombie.

But even if viewers had been able to follow the stories, they would have had a hard time suspending disbelief long enough to enjoy them. The premise—that an explosion on the dark side of the moon jolted it out of its orbit and sent it hurtling through space like a rocket ship—was preposterous. Besides, if an explosion like that ever occurred, it would send the moon hurtling *toward* Earth—not *away* from it.

"Space: 1999" did have one redeeming feature: its model work and special effects were more spectacular than anything previously made for TV. But as we've repeatedly seen in sf, visual tricks never compensate for a lack of quality in other areas.

In one episode of "Space: 1999", Landau announced: "We're sitting on the biggest bomb ever made." And as *TV Guide* added, "In a show like this, that's one line they should have avoided at any price."

BACKGROUND

In the late twentieth century, man established a tiny colony of 311 scientists and researchers on the moon. The colony was called Moon Base Alpha. But on Sept. 9, 1999, a freak accident in the moon's nuclear waste dumps created a new form of radiation that literally blasted it out of its orbit around Earth, sending it hurtling across the solar system. It passed through a black hole and is now lost in space. The colony's limited resources will soon be depleted, so the weary travelers are searching for a habitable planet that they can colonize. As they speed through the galaxy, they encounter many bizarre scientific phenomena and unusual alien life forms.

MAIN CAST:
• **Comdr. John Koenig** (Martin Landau): Stern, competent moon base commander.

• **Dr. Helena Russell** (Barbara Bain): In charge of medical affairs, strives to make Koenig more human.
• **Victor Bergman** (Barry Morse): Scientific genius with an electronic heart.
• **Maya** (Catherine Schell): Last survivor of the planet Psychon, a metamorph capable of changing forms.
• **Tony Verdeshi** (Tony Anholt): Koenig's right-hand man.
• **Alan Carter** (Nick Tate): Chief pilot.

FLASHBACK

KOENIG [addressing the people of Moon Base Alpha]: "As you know, we have been totally cut off from Earth. If we try to go back, we may fail. Therefore, in my judgment, we do not try."

KOENIG [dramatically, after Alan's ship has lost touch with Moon Base]: "Victor, if you're trying to tell me I made the wrong decision, tell me that. If you're trying to tell me I'm wasting my time trying to reach Alan out there through that radiation cloud, tell me that. But if you're telling me that you don't think Alan is ali-i-ive out there ... then I don't wanna hear it!"

"1999"'s fantastic pre-*Star Wars* effects were the creations of SFX director Brian Johnson and model-maker Martin Bower. More than fifty intricate spaceship models were built in two years. (Photo courtesy ITC Entertainment, Inc.)

CRITICS' COMMENTS

"Barbara Bain and Martin Landau ... were woefuly miscast in this. You couldn't identify with them—they were very remote, very cold....Ironically, you'd expect people at the forefront of a real space mission—scientists, mathematicians, etc.—not to be terribly warm, lively human beings. Yet for purposes of fiction and entertainment, that type of character doesn't have a whole lot of appeal."
—**Sharon Webb**, *SF Writer*

"You could never understand what any of the actors were saying. They all had world class mumbles. And you lost half of the dialogue. Barbara Bain's idea of showing shock or surprise was to step back two paces and look dumb. She did that at least three times an episode."
—**Nancy Kress**, *SF Writer*

"Maya is my favorite alien. She's the only woman who ever looked sexy in sideburns."
—**Michael Dougan**, *San Francisco Examiner*

"There was no levity in the series at all—it took itself very seriously—which just made me laugh harder. Like their silver clothing; for what reason? Why is everyone wearing silver clothing with shoulder pads and chevrons on their shoulders?"
—**David Jones,**
Columbus Dispatch

"Logically, when the nuclear reactors on the dark side of the moon go off, the moon should go flying into Cleveland—not into space. In fact, if it *did* smack into Cleveland, that would be an interesting story."
—**Joel Pisetzner,**
N.J. Bergen Record

Photo courtesy ITC Entertainment, Inc.

"It was a good effort ... 'Space 1999' was a pioneer. It was the first big-budget space TV show since 'Star Trek,' and it ushered in a whole new generation of special effects."
—**Harry Castleman**, *Watching TV*

"Nothing made any sense. ... The characters were basically running around like rats in a box, and I got tired of waiting for them to start gnawing on each other."
—**David Schow**, *The Outer Limits: The Official Companion*

BUCK ROGERS IN THE 25TH CENTURY

Buck Rogers made his debut in a 1928 edition of Amazing Stories magazine. He appeared in a popular comic strip from 1931 to 1956, and as a TV hero twice—once in a 1950 series, and then twenty-nine years later in "Buck Rogers in the 25th Century." The contemporary version ran from September 20, 1979, to April 16, 1981.

Frankly, "Buck Rogers" isn't as consistently bad as some of the other shows on this list. It wasn't a great series, but it never took itself seriously—so it could be fun, in a mindless sort of way. "At its best," says one critic, "it was escapist entertainment on the level of a mediocre "Star Trek" episode."

But when it was bad, it was horrible. Buck came across as a beefy, smirking frat boy with a Mouseketeer IQ. And the special effects, though obviously expensive, made futuristic technology look clunky and boring instead of sleek and innovative. As for Wilma—well, she looked so good in a spacesuit that it didn't matter whether she could act or not.

Worst of all, though, was Twiki the robot, an insufferable C3PO ripoff that didn't even deserve to exist as an *idea*. Whoever created that dish-headed, vibrating-voiced embarrassment probably should have been arrested for assaulting science fiction with a deadly weapon.

But ultimately, the reason this show wound up second on the "All-Time Worst" list has as much to do with its name as with its content. Buck Rogers was one of the most important characters in sf history. In the early 1930s—long before most people were thinking about rockets or TV—Buck's newspaper comic strip popularized the concepts of space travel and sophisticated technology. In fact, it was responsible for inspiring sf greats like Ray Bradbury, who was nine years old when he first read "Buck Rogers."

So when Glen Larson took on the project of updating the lanky space hero for TV, he also acquired the responsibility of upholding the character's integrity. But he didn't come close. Producer Leslie Stevens explained the Larson approach this way: "Buck is supposed to be so loose and fun-loving that he breaks Wilma down, teaches her how to enjoy life. ... He wants to boogie." To *boogie*? Buck Rogers? For longtime fans, that was heresy.

BACKGROUND

Capt. Buck Rogers, an American astronaut, took off from Earth in 1987 in a deep-space probe called *Ranger 3*. A freak mishap put him in suspended animation, and after floating around space for about five hundred years, his shuttle was recovered by Princess Ardala and her flagship *Draconia*. Revived, Buck escaped to Earth—where he discovered that the world he knew had

been wiped out in a holocaust four hundred years earlier. In the new high-tech society that evolved, Buck's old-fashioned American know-how made him a hero, the top pilot in the galaxy.

MAIN CAST:
•**Buck Rogers** (Gil Gerard): The 533-year-old All-American hero.
•**Col. Wilma Deering** (Erin Gray): Commander of Earth's defense; Buck's girlfriend.
•**Twiki** (Felix Silla): Buck's robot.

•**Dr. Huer** (Tim O'Connor): Earth's top scientist.
•**Dr. Theopolis** (Eric Server): A computer being helping run Earth.
•**Hawk** (Tom Christopher): Buck's friend, a half-human, half-bird.
•**Dr. Goodfellow** (Wilfred Hyde-White): Brainy, eccentric scientist.
•**Princess Ardala** (Pamela Hensley): Leader of the evil Draconians.
•**Kane** (Henry Silva/Michael Ansara): Ardala's henchman.
•**Admiral Asimov** (Jay Garner): Commander of the *Searcher*.

FLASHBACK

BUCK: "Are you busy later tonight?"
WILMA [eagerly]: "No."
BUCK: "That's too bad. I am."

BUCK [to a starship commander]: "If you call that interfering, there's something wrong with your Funk and Wagnall's."

TWIKI: "I always knew you were innocent, Buck. It's robotic intuition."
BUCK: "Robotic intuition?"
TWIKI: "Yeah. It's like female intuition, only more mechanical."

WILMA: "Buck, I want you to know something. No matter how this thing turns out, there's no man I've ever respected more."

Wilfred Hyde-White, a distinguished English actor, played Dr. Goodfellow for a year. His assessment of the show: "An illegitimate child of 'Battlestar Galactica.'"

CRITICS' COMMENTS

"The booming splendors of 'Buck Rogers' have become a bit monotonous. ... Yet the comic book cheekiness is rather entertaining. Gil Gerard has an insipid grin that might have been inked in by Roy Lichtenstein, and Erin Gray's tarty stride reminds you of every terrible actress who's ever tried to steal a scene with her hips. ... The actors have a foolish good time, and so do we."
—*Village Voice*, **original review, Oct. 8, 1979**

"Gil Gerard wasn't bad, but let's face it—do you believe that this guy has the scientific training it would take to pilot spaceships around the galaxy? He may be able to find his joy stick, but that's about it."
—**R.D. Heldenfels,** *Schenectady Gazette*

"That stupid robot was beneath contempt. An insult to all nonliving things."
—**Tom Shales,** *Washington Post*

"They took one of the only good female characters and made her more backward ... than she would be even in *this* age. [Wilma Deering] was supposed to be a military officer, and yet ... the producers kept telling [Erin Gray] not to be 'authoritarian.' That went beyond silliness. It was insulting."
—**C.J. Cherryh,** *SF Writer*

"They made no attempt to either extrapolate a realistic future or to create an imaginative one. But they did occasionally have moments of high camp. I give them credit for that."
—**Nancy Kress,** *SF Writer*

Henry Silva played Killer Kane, Buck's nemesis, for a year.

"It was sort of this retro-future, old and unoriginal. ... It tried to wear a spacesuit, but it looked more like a zoot suit."
—**Duane Dudek,** *Milwaukee Sentinel*

"If this is the future, then I want out."
—**Ken Hoffman,** *Houston Post*

GALACTICA 1980

The real Lorne Greene on planet Earth. "Galactica 1980" lasted for half a season, from January 27, 1980, to May 4, 1980. There were six episodes in nine weekly one-hour segments.

"Galactica 1980" was Part II of the "Battlestar Galactica" saga. Could the most expensive flop in history make a comeback six months after its demise—as a

midseason replacement for two sitcoms? Did anyone care?

Actually, most people didn't even realize that "Galactica 1980" was separate from the original "Battlestar" in the first place. But after "Battlestar" was canceled, ABC put its elaborate (and expensive) models into storage and secretly planned to use them again. "All we were told," said a special effects man at Universal, "was to keep the miniatures of 'Galactica' in good shape and under lock and key, that they were likely to be needed."

Behind the scenes the show's creator, Glen Larson, was lobbying for a second chance, too. "To an awful lot of people," Larson explained, "[the show] was very special. It had a life of its own. So we just kept pushing the thing." ABC eventually agreed. They commissioned a three-hour return, with a new premise: the Galacticans had ended their quest and arrived on Earth. For some reason, they dumped all the original characters *except* Lorne Greene.

"Galactica 1980" was showcased for three consecutive weeks beginning on January 27, 1980, and did so well that ABC instructed Larson to prepare it as a series ... to debut *four weeks later*! "We thought they were mad," Larson sighed a few months later, "and we *know* we were insane for having taken the job."

The series was a mess, thrown together so haphazardly that it couldn't even attract diehard "Battlestar Galactica" fans. "Many ... merely thought of 'Galactica 1980' as a bastard child," *Starlog* reported. After nine weeks, the series was put to rest. Today it's remembered—reluctantly—as a monument to irrelevance in science fiction TV.

BACKGROUND

In a continuation of "Battlestar Galactica," the Galacticans finally arrive at the long-lost planet Earth. But rejoicing turns to shock when they realize that Earth is technologically backward and its people are sitting ducks for their enemies, the robot Cylons. *Galactica* bypasses Earth, drawing the Cylons away from it, then sends emissaries to the

planet to force-feed new technology to its scientists so the planet can defend itself—and the Galacticans—against the Cylons. Survival of the human race depends on it.

MAIN CAST:
•**Cmdr. Adama** (Lorne Greene): Still the space messiah.
•**Capt. Troy** (Kent McCord): Adama's adopted grandson; chief emissary to Earth.

•**Lt. Dillon** (Barry Van Dyke): Troy's friend and partner.
•**Jamie Hamilton** (Robyn Douglass): Newswoman helping Troy and Dillon. The only Earthling who knows about *Galactica.*
•**Dr. Zee** (Robbie Risk/Patrick Stuart): 13-year-old genius coordinating the plan to advance Earth.
•**Col. Boomer** (Herb Jefferson, Jr.): *Galactica's* executive officer.
•**Xaviar** (Richard Lynch): Renegade member of the Council of Twelve.

FLASHBACK

THREE "GREAT GALACTICAN MOMENTS":
• In the second episode, "The Super Scouts," Lt. Dillon inadvertently robs a bank. He has to turn invisible to avoid getting thrown in jail.
• In the third episode, "Spaceball," the Galactican children wind up at a "baseball camp for underprivileged kids."
• In the fourth episode, "The Night the Cylons Landed," two Cylons thumb a ride with an Earth couple. They get away undetected because the couple just happens to be on their way to a Halloween party.

WHISTLING IN THE DARK:
• "I don't think that we're limited with 'Galactica 1980,' " said "Galactica" creator Glen Larson, who wrote all but one of the teleplays for the show. "We still have the opportunity to go anywhere in space we want."

• "There are opportunities to do some really interesting science fiction concepts right here on [Earth] where there's a much larger audience-identification factor," Larson declared.

A plastic model kit of the Galactica.

CRITICS' COMMENTS

"You mean they made it to Earth? I didn't know—by that time I wasn't watching anymore."
—**Robert Bianco,** *Pittsburgh Press*

"Now we've got 'The Beverly Hillbillies' with lasers. I just don't buy it. I didn't buy those guys when they were up there—how am I going to buy them when they're down here?"
—**R.D. Heldenfels,** *Schenectady Gazette*

"The reason I hated the revival more than the original is that they had the nerve to do it again. I mean, it's like a vampire—you want the stake to keep it dead. My God—what if there had been a 'Galactica 1981?' It's a frightening thought. ... Of course, by the time they arrived on Earth, nobody was watching—nobody *should* have been watching. They didn't have to arrive anywhere."
—**David Bianculli,** *New York Post*

"The stories were a complete waste of time. 'Battlestar Galactica' at least had a few interesting attempts. But what I see in 'Galactica 1980' is a studio amortizing its sets and its name. This is television as a merchandising ploy."
—**Michael Cassutt,** *SF/ TV Writer*

" 'Galactica 1980' departed science fiction and went over into what I call the 'Astral Annie' field, for people who are into the significance of pyramids and spoon-bending."
—**C.J. Cherryh,** *SF Writer*

A pair of Cylon dolls.

"When the Cylon warriors came down and blasted Hollywood Boulevard, it was really just their ships matted over a sequence of footage from the film *Earthquake*. Every time a ray would zap out, it would be hitting a building at the moment the structure was collapsing in the original film. Rather clever. They made it look as though they'd done a whole lot of special effects, when actually they'd only done a little bit."
—**Douglas Menville,** *Author /SF Critic*

THE POWERS OF MATTHEW STAR

Peter Barton was lucky to get out of "Matthew Star" alive. In 1981 he was filming a scene in which he was tied to a chair. He fell backwards, onto some magnesium flares, and received 2nd- and 3rd-degree burns. Fortunately Lou Gossett, who was also in the scene, was there to save Barton. The show was delayed an entire season while Barton recovered in the hospital.

This show is the flip side of "The Wild, Wild West"—a TV hybrid that *didn't* work. Producer Harve Bennett combined high school, adventure, and science fiction, and came up with a Donny Osmond clone from outer space who was both a government agent and the quarterback of the football team. Well, it's original; you've got to say that much.

As a comedy, "Matthew Star" might have worked. Every adolescent sometimes feels that he or she is from another planet; the producers could have exploited that and given the term "alienated teenager" a whole new meaning. Then they might have had people laughing *with* the show instead of at it.

But as a "straight" program, it was just ludicrous. A prince arrives from outer space and … enrolls in an American high school? That made no sense at all. Was he worried that he couldn't get a job back on his home planet without a diploma, or what?

And the "companion" bit was hard to swallow. Matthew, an attractive teenage student, just happened to be living with this big dude named Walt—who was also his science teacher and football coach. Even the innocents in a town like Crestview might have been a little suspicious about an arrangement like that.

There were plenty of other rough spots. Matthew looked too old; he was too confused; he was too good-looking. But the real problems began earlier, with the premise. This show misfired on the drawing board; the truth is, poor Matthew never really had a chance to survive on Earth.

BACKGROUND

Matthew Star's parents, the rulers of a world called Quadris, were overthrown by tyrants. To prevent their son from being captured, they sent him to Earth in the care of Walt Shephard. Walt's instructions were: help Matthew develop his powers of telepathy and telekenesis so that he can return to Quadris to lead a revolution; and defend him against alien assassins. Walt and Matt arrive in a town called Crestview and take up residence together, posing as guardian and ward. Matthew enrolls in Crestview High School and Walt gets a job as the football coach/science teacher. Eventually, Matt develops the power of astral projection and drops out of high school to become a US secret agent.

MAIN CAST:
•**Matthew Star** (Peter Barton): teenager from another planet, captain of the football team.
•**Walt Shephard** (Lou Gossett, Jr.): Matt's friend, surrogate father, and mentor; a loyal subject of the Quadrisian royal family.
•**Pam Elliott** (Amy Steel): Matthew's high school girlfriend.
•**Chip Frye** (Bob Alexander): Matthew's high-school buddy.
•**Major Wymore** (James Karen): Matthew's government contact.

FLASHBACK

"Of course there's no subtle way to deal with the NBC series that made its debut last Friday. Dumb is the word that describes 'The Powers of Matthew Star.' Brief is the word that describes its probable life expectancy at 8 P.M. opposite 'Dukes of Hazzard.' More than anything, 'Matthew Star' dabbles in science fiction. It sure doesn't dabble in entertainment....The real UFO in this Harve Bennett-produced awful mess is [Lou] Gossett. Having him in 'Matthew Star' is like having Rudolf Nuryev square dance on 'Hee Haw.' Hee Hawrible."
—*Los Angeles Times*,
Sept. 22, 1982

Lou Gossett felt that "Matthew Star" had merit and was on the verge of becoming popular when it was canceled. It aired on NBC for only one season—from September 17, 1982, to September 11, 1983. It was an hour-long show.

CRITICS' COMMENTS

"I felt sorry for Lou Gosset, who was trapped in that monstrosity. I mean, the guy's got too much talent to be working in a show like that."
—**Michael Duffy**, *Detroit Free Press*

"It was an attempt to combine the appeal of a comic book superhero with a teenage hook. David Cassidy meets Superman."
—**Michael Hill**, *Baltimore Evening Sun*

"It began as 'Star Child,' and then it was the 'Powers of David Star,' and then it was 'The Powers of Matthew Star'—and that just shows the misplaced priorities. Here they are screwing around with titles, and they have a show that's a mess. … At no time was it ever believable. You couldn't accept the premise, the character made no sense, and the kid seemed to be a candidate for teen suicide. He was constantly troubled by the powers he had. I was a teenager, you were a teenager—we know that at least at *some* stage, you'd find it kind of charming and maybe a little bit of fun that you had these powers. But this kid was just constantly troubled that he could do things that no one else could. There was nothing about this show that rang true"
—**Tom Jicha**, *Miami News*

"They had a 25-year-old man playing a high-school boy. That was bad enough, but then they had to surround him with a bunch of adults about his own age and have *them* playing high-school kids too, so he didn't look too out of context. In one wonderful episode, the children were all waiting for the school bus, and here were these people in their 20s, each with a handful of books under their arms, getting aboard a yellow bus to go to school. … It was a ridiculous show."
—**R.K. Shull**, *Indianapolis News*

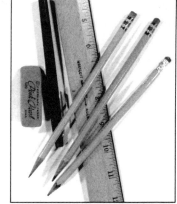

An unsolved mystery: Did Matthew bring his school supplies from Quadris?

"NBC really was in a desperate state then, and this program showed it."
—**Rick Du Brow**, *Los Angeles Herald Examiner*

BATTLESTAR GALACTICA

Before it was launched, "Battlestar Galactica" was hyped as the most expensive, most elaborate, most exciting television series ever. It was an historic event: not only was a major studio finally committing the resources to create a first-rate modern science fiction show, the whole sf genre, it seemed, was finally coming into its own. It was all the more disappointing, then, when Universal's mighty labors brought forth this tiresome, totally unimaginative Biblical space opera.

Ok, you have to give them *some* credit; they were obviously trying.

But one has to wonder what kind of logic was behind the producers' major decisions regarding the program. Why, for example, did they cast Lorne Greene as a Battlestar Moses? He's a fine human being, an entertaining actor, a great father figure. But he'll always be Ben Cartwright to TV viewers—and dressing him up in robes just made him look funny.

With the rest of the crew, "Battlestar"'s creators gave us only stereotypes. Starbuck and what's-his-name were the Hardy Boys in space, the same uninspired good-guy caricatures we've been watching on TV for thirty-five years. Athena and Cassiopea were the tough-yet-sensitive women you'd find on any Western wagon train. It's baffling; all that money spent for scripts, and the writers couldn't even come up with one character who resembled a real human being.

Only the special effects, which were more spec-

An ad for the show's celebrated premiere, on Sept. 17, 1978. But it didn't live up to its promise. It was a one-season wonder that only lasted for 17 episodes. The final one aired on April 29, 1979.

tacular than anything ever attempted for TV, were noteworthy. And even that backfired. Effects aren't special if they're the only entertainment a program has to offer. Watching elaborate models go "poof" gets old in a hurry, especially when viewed on a small screen. "Battlestar Galactica" was able to recreate the look, but not the impact, of *Star Wars*. There's only one consolation here. After this magnificent failure, TV executives will never again believe that massive special effects can compensate for lack of plot and character development. We hope.

BACKGROUND

In the seventh millennium, A.D., a thousand-year war between twelve tribes of spacehumans and a race of robots called Cylons ended with treachery. As the two forces met in space to sign a peace treaty, the Cylons attacked and destroyed not only the humans' vessels, but also their home planets. Only one battlestar—*Galactica*—remained. It became the mother ship for all hu-

man survivors, the center of a rag-tag armada of space vessels fleeing their mortal foes. Now homeless, the survivors trek through space in *Galactica*, desperately fending off the pursuing Cylons as they seek the legendary "Golden Planet" of the thirteenth human tribe—Earth.

MAIN CAST:
•**Cmdr. Adama** (Lorne Greene): Patriarch of *Galactica*.
• **Capt. Apollo** (Richard Hatch): Adama's son, commander of the

Squadron of Viper fighters.
•**Lt. Starbuck** (Dirk Benedict): Lovable scoundrel, ace pilot.
•**Sgt. Boomer** (Herb Jefferson): Fighter pilot.
•**Lt. Athena** (Maren Jensen): Adama's daughter, pilot, communications officer; in love with Starbuck.
•**Count Baltar** (John Colicos): Human traitor who joined the Cylons.
•**Boxey** (Noah Hathaway): Apollo's adopted son.
•**Cassiopea** (Laurette Sprang): Medical technician.

FLASHBACK

ADAMA [solemnly]: "Let the record show that on the first contact with the people from Terra, my weapon is set on stun."

ADAMA [solemnly]: "They hate us with every fiber of their existence."

STARBUCK: "Will you cut the felgercarb and get me outta here?"

ADAMA: [solemnly]: "Cylons lured me into their deceptions once. Never again."

Dirk Benedict, the real "Battlestar" survivor. Of all the actors and actresses who starred in this ill-fated sf series, Dirk Benedict came out in the best shape. He went on to play Face in "The A-Team," a Top Ten hit, just three years after "Galactica" was cancelled.

CRITICS' COMMENTS

"The actors here are narcissistically bland—a pride of Hollywood pretty boys. They shoot fast, fly fast, and brush between meals. ... [And] despite the millions spent on special effects, there's no joy or terror or beauty to the destruction on 'Battlestar Galactica.' "
—*Village Voice*, **original review, Sept. 25, 1978**

"I never had any idea of who the characters were; they tended to blend into one. I mean, which women were which? And who was seeing whom? And who was who's brother? And who was the son? They all seemed interchangeable."
—**Robert Bianco,** *Pittsburgh Press*

"I know they tried to do their best ... but as the season went on it got worse and worse. The problem was that these people did not have a heroic mission. They were running away from the Cylons—they weren't running *to* something, they weren't searching out something. The starship *Enterprise* always had bold, courageous, noble missions. 'Galactica' was 'Run like hell—we're being chased.' And that's cowardice. You can't make cowardice noble, no matter how hard you try."
—**David Gerrold,** *SF/TV Writer*

" 'Battlestar Galactica' is the worst science fiction show ever, considering what its promise and potential were. ... It followed on the heels of *Star Wars* and 'Star Trek,' so it had a chance to use *Star Wars* technology with 'Star Trek' TV values, and didn't do either. Lorne Greene's performance wasn't nearly as good as his Alpo commercials; the stories were juvenile; and having the special effects reduced to the small screen just made them look pedestrian."
—**Ed Siegel,** *Boston Globe*

"I'm sure the purists blanch at these things, but all television has to be homogenized, so why shouldn't science fiction be? ... It's amazing that 'Battlestar Galactica' looked as good as it did."
—**Tom Shales,** *Washington Post*

"Battlestar Exlaxia."
—**Marvin Kitman,** *Long Island Newsday*

LOST IN SPACE

Neither Dr. Smith nor the Robot were originally part of the cast. But just before filming the pilot, story editor Tony Newman decided to add them, to increase plot possibilities. Dr. Smith was a temporary addition—he was going to be killed off after the sixth episode—but he got so much fan mail that producer Irwin allen decided to make him the star of the show instead. "Lost in Space" lasted for three years, from September 15, 1965, to September 11, 1968. Eighty-three episodes were filmed.

It's another typical day for the Robinson family on asteroid X. Mom's in the spaceship doing laundry in a machine that not only washes, but folds and bags everyone's clothes. Dad's taking readings of the planet's surface with Don and Judy. Penny's out picking flowers. And Will and the Robot are keeping an eye on Dr. Smith, the sniveling creep who got them into this mess to begin with. They're all waiting for the "Monster of the Week" to show up. What will it be today? A walking, talking carrot? A stunt man with a sheet over his head? An actor with his face painted gold? It could be anything—as long as it doesn't cost too much. Once, it's said, when producer Irwin Allen was informed that an alien's spaceship was budgeted at $10,000, he turned red in the face and screamed, "Let him walk!"

Actually, "Lost in Space," the first space opera of the space age, was a decent show in its first season. But it fell victim to the ratings wars. In January 1966, ABC stuck "Batman" into the slot opposite "Lost in Space" and clobbered it in the Neilsens. Even June Lockhart admitted that her kids had defected to the Caped Crusader. When Irwin Allen tried to emulate "Batman"'s camp humor, he got in over his head—and that was the end of the Robinsons. "Lost in Space" went totally out of control, getting sillier by the week until it became unwatchable—even insulting—to many of its fans.

BACKGROUND

By 1997, overpopulation was strangling Earth; Man's only hope of survival was to colonize other worlds. So American scientists built the *Jupiter 2* spaceship and selected the Robinson family to be space pioneers. Their destination was Alpha Centauri, but they never got there. A "foreign agent" (Dr. Smith) slipped aboard and reprogrammed the Robot to destroy the ship in flight. But the agent was trapped on board, and when the robot went berserk, he had to wake the crew. They stopped the robot, but not before he'd destroyed the ship's controls, marooning them in space.

MAIN CAST:
•**John Robinson** (Guy Williams): A 40-year-old astrophysicist.
•**Maureen Robinson** (June Lockhart): His biochemist-wife.
•**Judy Robinson** (Marta Kristen): Their beautiful eldest daughter.
•**Penny Robinson** (Angela Cartwright): An 11-year-old studying geology.
•**Will Robinson** (Billy Mumy): A 9-year-old electronics whiz.
•**Major Don West** (Mark Goddard): An expert in celestial geology; Judy's boyfriend.
•**Robot** (Bob May, Dick Tufeld).
•**Dr. Zachary Smith** (Jonathan Harris): The sniveling spy.

FLASHBACK

[Dr. Smith is transported to another dimension, where he meets a "devilish" alien]

SMITH: "Where am I, all these rocks and the fire. And that dreadful smell of brimstone. Oh no! It can't be! That kindly, noble Zachary Smith could end up in this infernal place. It's not fair. Oh dear!"

ALIEN: "Well, Zachary, so you finally got here."

SMITH: "Good heavens! ... Where am I?"

ALIEN: "Now who the devil do you think I am, and where in Hades do you think you are?"

SMITH: "The Devil? Hades? Oh the pain, the pain!"

"The first season I feel very good about," says Bill "Will Robinson" Mumy. "After that, I can't say it was a quality science fiction show any more."

CRITICS' COMMENTS

"The Perils of Pauline have been put into a split-level saucer and 'Lost in Space' is a surefire winner for young viewers and probably will amuse senior devotees of science fiction. ... The show is the first crop of throroughly professional corn to be reaped from the exploits of the National Aeronautics and Space Administration."
— ***New York Times***, original review, Sept. 16, 1965

"Dr. Smith was this dumb SOB and every week he got them into trouble. After about two or three weeks of that, I'd kick him out the air lock."
—**David Gerrold,**
SF/TV Writer

"What makes it a lousy show? That's like saying, 'What made Orson Wells big?' Let's start with Dr. Smith. He's a despicable, weasly, unprincipled character, and not a very likable actor. So who's going to want to watch him?"
—**Gordon Javna,**
Tough TV

"It wasn't just that they took a reasonable concept and ran it into the ground—they took a reasonable concept and then didn't do anything with it at *all*. They used the same plot over and over again."
—**Craig Miller,**
SF Publicist/ TV writer

Other cast-members were furious that Jonathan Harris got most of the good lines in "Lost in Space," but Harris didn't seem to mind. "Happy as a clam, I am," he exclaimed to a reporter.

"They never changed the set; whenever they landed on a planetoid or an asteroid, it was always the same asteroid. Look, I can only watch the same rock so many times."
—**Tom Jicha,**
Miami News

THE MAN FROM ATLANTIS

When he auditioned for the show, Duffy hadn't swum a stroke in five years. "I didn't even have a bathing suit," he told TV Guide in 1977. "I had to audition in my underwear."

Imagine, for a moment, that the last survivor of an underwater civilization washed up on a beach. What would he be like?

Would he be a webfooted boy scout, with impeccable manners and a pleasing disposition? Would he speak perfect English? Would he volunteer to become a secret agent for Uncle Sam? Would he look like Patrick Duffy?

The answer to all of the above is "probably not"— which is the fundamental reason that "The Man from Atlantis" was a failure. The producers took a viable science fiction concept and sanitized it. Their "Atlantean" seemed more like a ROTC volunteer than a renegade amphibian.

It's not Duffy's fault, though; he wore the swim trunks, not the pants, in this operation. He could learn to wriggle through the water like a human fish, but not even Olivier could have done anything with the scripts he was handed.

In retrospect, it's a safe guess that the producers were using Atlantis to introduce a waterlogged "Six Million Dollar Man." The previous season, both Lee Majors and Lindsay Wagner made bionic leaps into the Top 15 shows of the year, and NBC probably dreamed of floating their weird new superhero into the upper reaches of the Neilsens, too. But it didn't work. "The Man From Atlantis" came off like a "Man from UNCLE" mutation, complete with its comical villains and superscientific doomsday devices, but without its engaging personalities and witty repartee. So when the silt settled, "The Man from Atlantis" was just another also-swam.

BACKGROUND

An underwater disturbance uncovered the last survivor of Atlantis, who happened to be a handsome male. He washed to shore unconscious, perhaps dying. But luckily, he was found on a California beach by a beautiful woman naval doctor. She christened him Mark Harris and nursed him back to health. Later, after he'd recovered, she explained that she worked for the Foundation for Oceanic Research—a West Coast facility dedicated to furthering human knowledge of the sea. He agreed to assist her, exploring the ocean in the supersub *Cetacean*. He also took on assignments for the US government whenever evil scientists or aliens threatened.

MAIN CAST:
• **Mark Harris** (Patrick Duffy): The last Atlantean; has webbed hands and feet, gills instead of lungs, superstrength on land and superspeed in water; must be immersed in water every twelve hours.
• **Dr. Elizabeth Merrill** (Belinda Montgomery): Mark's co-worker at the Foundation for Oceanic Research; saved his life.
• **C.W. Crawford** (Alan Fudge): The director of the Foundation for Oceanic Research.
• **Mr. Schubert** (Victor Buono): Mark's nemesis, a mad scientist who'd love to dissect him.

FLASHBACK

MARK [revealing his reason for hanging around with human beings]: "I have not learned enough."

MARK [as he prepares to return to the ocean]: "I'm going to tell you something now, and I want you to listen. And I'm going to call you 'Elizabeth.'"
ELIZABETH: [waiting for the big goodbye] "Well, what?"
MARK: "Keep your ears clean, Elizabeth."

SHUBERT: "A water-breathing man! What a waste!"

Patrick Duffy is a huge star in mainland China—not because of his role in "Dallas," but because "The Man from Atlantis" was the first American entertainment TV program ever shown there. In America, however, the show ran for only one season—from September 22, 1977, to July 25, 1978—and most viewers never saw it.

CRITICS' COMMENTS

"When 'The Man From Atlantis' premiered last season as a set of two-hour movies, the shows had several pluses to commend them....Now [it's] back as a series...but few will recognize their old friend despite the fact he's still clad in the same unattractive swimsuit....As mysteriously as it arrived on the scene, the quality of the originals has disappeared. The script is a silly excercise in technical jargon and blinking lights....[It's] directed with one hand in the cookie jar, the other in the playpen, with the resulting hour of interest only to preteens."
—*Daily Variety*, **original review, Oct 24 , 1978**

"When Patrick Duffy reappeared on 'Dallas' in the shower scene, I said, 'Look down—he probably came up through the plumbing.' "
—**Dusty Saunders,** *Rocky Mountain News*

"It was supposed to be an adaptation of *The Submariner*, a comic-book character who rules Atlantis, for television. But while the Submariner was every bit as arrogant as you'd expect an undersea ruler to be, the Man from Atlantis was an even nicer guy than Bobby Ewing. He was too good to be true, too stupid to be entertaining, and too noble to be tolerated."
—**David Bianculli,** *New York Post*

"Instead of exploring the legend of Atlantis—where he's coming from, what he's doing—we get all these little adventures. In one episode a scientist is trying to

Victor Buono as Schubert

figure out how the Atlantean can stay out of the water for so long ... and it ends up with the kind of chase you would've seen in 'The Fugitive.' What about Atlantis? He could get chased on 'Dragnet.' I thought this was supposed to be science fiction."
—**David Heath,** *President, N3F*

"It was all wet."

—**Ken Hoffman,** *Houston Post*

THE STARLOST

"The Starlost" was syndicated in 1973; there were sixteen episodes. The inspiration for the show was a Robert A. Heinlein story called "Universe." Interesting switch: On TV, Devon and Rachel (above) learn the fantastic secret of Earthship Ark in the opening episode of this hour-long series. In the original novel, the discovery that they're on a spaceship, not a planet, was the climax at the end.

Harlan Ellison is one of the best-known science fiction writers in America. So executives at CTV, the Canadian television company behind "The Starlost," assumed they'd engineered a coup when Ellison agreed to help them create a science fiction TV series.

But it didn't work out too well. Ellison decided they were butchering his creation and withdrew from the project. Then he recorded the whole unpleasant episode in his book *The Other Glass Teat.* Thus "The Starlost," which made nary a ripple on the American screen when it appeared as a syndicated series in 1972, gained the notoriety that landed it here.

Not that it doesn't deserve to be on the list. The characters' "adventures" in Earthship *Ark* were painfully tedious. In the early episodes, for example, they discovered the "Tube People," a society of nasty teenagers, and a pack of angry killer bees—a group of antagonists so boring that it made you wonder if Earth had really done anyone a favor by preserving the species. And *2001*'s Keir Dullea, in the lead role, was as dreary as his foes—which was particularly disappointing.

The show's most notable failure, however, came in its attempt to use videotape—years before the medium was perfected. Everything was shot on the same blue background, and the human figures looked as if they'd been cut out and pasted onto the screen. This wasn't just bad—it was actually distracting. Viewers found themselves so amazed by the cheap visual tricks that they completely lost track of the plots—which, according to critics, was a blessing in disguise.

BACKGROUND

In 2285 A.D., Earth was faced with a catastrophe that threatened to destroy all life on the planet. To preserve the human race, the Committee of Scientists created Earthship *Ark*, an enormous "organic cluster of environmental domes called biospheres, looped to each other through tubular corridors for life

support communication." They filled it with the most desirable elements of life on Earth and sent it off hoping its inhabitants would ultimately find the solar system of a class-six star—which could support Earth life—and colonize there. However, now it is 2790 A.D., five hundred years later, and the *Ark*'s population is unaware they are on a spaceship. Only Devon, Rachel, and Garth have stumbled on the truth, and they want to learn more.

MAIN CAST:
- **Devon** (Keir Dullea): A poor farm boy who loves Rachel; flees home when he's sentenced to death for protesting the law forbidding him from marrying outside his class.
- **Rachel** (Gay Rowan): The beautiful young woman who escapes with Devon.
- **Garth** (Robin Ward): Rachel's ex-fiance; goes along with the pair because he wants to "protect" her from Devon.

FLASHBACK

ANNOUNCER: " 'The Starlost' … the incredible adventure of a giant spacecraft … carrying the survivors of a dead planet Earth on the most critical mission ever launched by man … An endless journey across the universe in search of a new world. Earthship *Ark* … hundreds of miles long. … A mammoth cluster of metal domes. … Each a separate community isolated from the others. In the countless generations that have lived and died since the launching of the *Ark*, everyone has forgotten that the Earth ever existed, forgotten the reason for their journey. …Unaware that they are streaking through the heavens in a man-made world."

Between jobs. After "Star Trek" left TV, but before it was resurrected in the movies, Walter "Chekov" Koenig took parts in shows like this one. In two episodes of "Starlost," he played an alien named Oro.

CRITICS' COMMENTS

"There wasn't one redeeming feature. Not one. The scripts were stupid, and to call the characters two-dimensional is to exaggerate by at least one dimension."

—**Nancy Kress,** *SF Writer*

"Rumor has it that at one point, they had a writers' strike and hired Canadian high school kids to write scripts—if so, it's understandable that the stories are pretty thin."

—**Dean Lambe,** *SF Writer*

"Once Harlan Ellison left the show, the writing degenerated. The show made no sense. And it had this music that kept playing all the time in the background, this rambling score that didn't seem connected to what was happening on the screen. It was like they had some guy playing the organ off camera and he was just sort of in his own world."

—**Marc Scott Zicree,** *The Twilight Zone Companion*

"It looked as if they didn't have any sets—like they'd done miniatures, videotaped them close up, and superimposed the characters in front of them. … I was so taken by the cheapness of production that I never knew what was going on in the story. "

—**F. Paul Wilson,** *SF Writer*

"I remember a toy that I had as a child called a *Vacu-Form* —you melted these little sheets of plastic on a griddle, flipped them over onto a mold and made little toys. It seemed that all the 'Starlost' sets were made on a *Vacu-Form*, two inches at a time, and then pasted together."

—**Peter Pautz,** *SF Writer*

Gay Rowan as Rachel.

"It was a noble attempt to have a 'wagon train to the stars,' but the problem was that they were limited to the spaceship—discovering what other societies were on it—and that made it boring. The drama and the stories were so dry that it had none of the life of 'Star Trek.' "

—**Gary H. Grossman,** *Author/TV producer*

VOYAGE TO THE BOTTOM OF THE SEA

And the hits keep coming: Captain Crane takes on...a clown? Despite its ludicrous plots, kids kept watching "Voyage." The hour-long show was one of the most popular first-run science fiction TV series ever, airing for four years. It debuted on September 14, 1964, and ended on September 15, 1968. There were 110 episodes.

Not every episode of "Voyage" belongs on the worst list; the series developed in three seperate stages, and only the last was intolerable.

It first surfaced as a 1961 kids' adventure film about a supersub, starring Walter Pidgeon and Joan Fontaine. Critics were generally kind and box office receipts good, so director Irwin Allen (backed by Groucho Marx) decided to spin it off into a TV series in 1964. That first season, filmed in black and white, is considered among Allen's best TV work.

But it was straight to the bottom from there.

During the next three seasons, the submarine *Seaview* was a weekly stopover for some of the silliest low-budget extraterrestrials who ever tried to conquer Earth. In one epsiode, six *wind-up toys* were sent by aliens to gain control of the sub. Production cost for the alien attack: about $20.

In another, Admiral Nelson's body was possessed by a hostile orchid. "Voyage" didn't need a special effects man that week; just a florist. And in my favorite, Vincent Price tried to replace each crew member with a sort of look-alike puppet. Why? Part of an alien attack, of course. Figure that one out.

The *Seaview* was supposedly manned by experienced sailors, but their lack of common sense made the boobs on Gilligan's Island look like geniuses. Nearly every week, someone or something hid in the air conditioning ducts.Yet none of the crew *ever* looked there. Didn't they remember last week's plot? Nope—they never learned. And apparently, neither did the show's writers.

BACKGROUND

Thirteen years in the future, the atomic supersub *Seaview* is created at the Nelson Institute of Marine Research in Santa Barbara, California, by Admiral Nelson. It is commissioned by the US government to conduct scientific research, but that's actually a cover for its real mission—combating threats to world peace from foreign countries

and alien invaders. The *Seaview* dives farther—4,450 feet—and travels faster than any other sub in history. It is equipped with mini-sub, diving bell, snowcat, and the flying sub, which converts for land or sea use.

MAIN CAST:
•**Ex-Admiral Harriman Nelson** (Richard Basehart): A scientific genius who designed and built the

Seaview, and now commands it.
•**Capt. Lee Crane** (David Hedison): Anapolis graduate, the youngest sub captain ever.
•**Executive Officer "Chip" Morton** (Robert Dowdell): Lee's right-hand man and close friend.
•**CPO Francis Sharkey** (Terry Becker): A regular Navy man who does most of the work, with the help of Kowalski and Patterson.
•**CPO Curly Jones** (Henry Kulky): The *Seaview*'s first CPO.

FLASHBACK

[The Van Allen radiation belt has caught fire, and the Seaview has been called in to help extinguish the blaze.]

NELSON: "I say we can stop the fire by exploding a nuclear device 3,000 miles in the air. This will blow the burning gases clear of the Earth's magnetic field."

SCIENTIST: "That sounds like a dangerous plan!"

SHARKEY: "We'll never know until we find out!"

NELSON [while the ship is being attacked]: "I think we'd better go down into my cabin and discuss this."

Every day was Halloween on the Seaview.

CRITICS' COMMENTS

In real life, Richard Basehart wouldn't go near a sub. "Who? Me? Go down in a real submarine? Never!" he responded to a reporter in 1965. "My god, I get claustrophobia."

"The most amazing thing about this show is how long it lasted. As bad as it was, there were still enough people who watched it regularly for NBC to carry it for four consecutive years."
—**Michael Dougan, *San Francisco Examiner***

"The first season of 'Voyage to the Bottom of the Sea' wasn't nearly as bad as what came after. I think a lot of people have forgotten that. They started out with a plausible action/adventure series with a futuristic touch. They ended up with crazy science fiction. Starting in the second season, it seemed like every week they were fighting a giant squid or an alien. It got more and more ridiculous."
—**Mark Dawidziak, *Akron Beacon-Journal***

"People call it 'The Voyage to the Bottom of the Brain.'"
—**Andy Porter, *Science Fiction Chronicle***

"They should've called it 'Lurching at the Bottom of the Sea.'"
—**Sharon Webb, *SF Writer***

"They must've had a $1 budget for special effects. Someone got a good deal on something that flashes sparks—and then they had to use it every week, all the time. The only suspense was waiting for them to tilt the camera and have these guys run back and forth as the submarine was supposedly being beaten back and forth by some alien force."
—**Michael Duffy, *Detroit Free Press***

"I love submarine stories. I have claustrophobia, so I get my kicks that way."
—**Tom Shales, *Washington Post***

IT'S ABOUT TIME

Hector and Mac, the astronauts that time forgot. "It's About Time" ran for one season, from September 11, 1966, to September 3, 1967. Twenty-six episodes were filmed.

Producer Sherwood Schwartz, who was enjoying a surprising success with "Gilligan's Island" in 1966, had every reason to believe that the American public would buy anything he created. To prove it, he dispatched a pair of dimwitted astronauts back to the Stone Age to join their first cousins, the sitcom Neanderthals, and waited for viewers to discover them all on CBS.

In real life, the cavemen probably would have torn these two bumbling spacemen limb from limb and eaten them. Unfortunately, this didn't happen. Instead, they were befriended by a pair of aging comics wearing bearskin rugs and had to spend the next three months—along with the audience— trying to figure out how to escape back into the twentieth century.

They finally did it in January 1967. Schwartz and CBS were disappointed by the show's low ratings, but still weren't ready to give up. So as the second half of the season began, the astronauts broke the time barrier again. But after landing in LA, they discovered they weren't alone—the aging Neanderthal comics had thumbed a ride into the '60s. Did the astronauts share this scientific miracle with the rest of the world ? No. Hec and Mac tried to hide the cavemen in their apartment. Smart move.

Then, when the show was canceled a few months later, Schwartz had the nerve to speculate that it was because he was—are you ready for this—ahead of his time! Now *that's* science fiction.

BACKGROUND

In 1966 a NASA rocket carrying two astronauts into space somehow breaks through the time barrier. The two dazed Americans land unharmed in a swamp, and after saving a caveboy named Breer, they realize they're stuck in the Stone Age. Tough luck. Meanwhile, the Cave People think they're evil spirits and plan to kill them—until

Breer's father, Gronk, intervenes. The astronauts' lives are spared, and an uneasy truce with the Boss and his tribe is struck while our heroes search for copper to repair their rocket. They finally find it and blast off for the 20th century— unaware that Gronk and his family are stowaways.

Back in Los Angeles, the two astronauts stash the Neanderthals in Mac's apartment and give them lessons in twentieth century survival.

MAIN CAST:
- **Hector** (Jack Mullaney): A stranded astronaut.
- **Mac** (Frank Aletter): The other stranded astronaut.
- **Gronk** (Joe E. Ross): Hec and Mac's ally, the head of the time-traveling Cave clan.
- **Shad** (Imogene Coca): Cave-wife.
- **Mlor** (Mary Grace): Cave-daughter.
- **Boss**: (Cliff Norton): The boss.
- **Clon** (Mike Mazurki): Tough guy.

It's TV theme song sing-along time. Ready? "It's about time, It's about space, It's about people in the strangest place ..."

FLASHBACK

"The characters are involved in adventures. As a result, the theme is stronger. I don't worry, 'Is the boss coming home for dinner?' I worry, 'Do they live or die?' I have a strong dramatic story told in a comedy way. It's life and death to those watching."

—**Executive Producer Sherwood Schwartz, 1966**

"Turn loose a band of cave dwellers, one with a massive club in hand, on a city boulevard, and you could write it yourself. Gronk, the massive savage, smashes a VW in the belief that it is a strange animal; when the rocking chair rocks, Imogene Coca lets out a scream, 'It's alive'; the fancy plumbing is smashed and floods the place; [and] the TV set is smashed as something evil."

—*Daily Variety*, Jan. 1967, **after the astronauts' return to their own time**

CRITICS' COMMENTS

"It's bad Saturday morning television with real people. Not even as good as 'The Flintstones' on a bad day. 'Gilligan's Island' meets 'The Flintstones,' and they both lose."

—**Michael Cassutt, SF/ TV Writer**

"It's a spoof just about on the level of the Neanderthals that they purported to poke fun at. There wasn't any characterization—it was slapstick. Looking for characterization in it is like trying to find Moliere in 'The Three Stooges.' It was a human cartoon. Even as a kid, my intelligence was insulted."

—**Jeff Borden, *Charlotte Observer***

" 'It's About Time' was a one-joke show that they tried to stretch and stretch, far beyond the breaking point. And then they tried to reverse the joke, and discovered that they had another one-joke show."

—**Jack Mingo, *The Couch Potato Handbook***

"It relied exclusively on mugging for its characterization. It was just making faces—Imogene Coca, Joe E. Ross—instead of trying to develop characters, they tried to see who could pull the funniest face. That's why I liked it as a kid, but in terms of science fiction it was insulting. Even to have this on the list of science fiction offerings is probably a real slap in the face to serious science fiction fans."

—**Joseph Walker, *Salt Lake City Deseret News***

" 'It's About Time' had one of the most pleasant theme songs of any TV show."

—**Ken Hoffman, *Houston Post***

The astronauts are confronted by the Cave Boss (Cliff Norton) and his right hand Neanderthal, Clon (Mike Mazurki). Against his better judgment—and ours—the Cave Boss decided not to kill them.

TV'S MOST POPULAR ALIEN
Leonard Nimoy accepted the part of Spock in the first "Star Trek" pilot not because he loved the idea of playing an alien, but because it was an opportunity for three consecutive weeks of work—the most he'd ever had in Hollywood. Critics in this poll voted him their favorite TV alien.

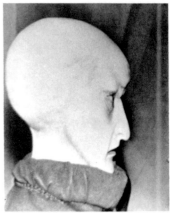

Balok.

The Klingon swine.

The "Salt Vampire."

Here are several of the critics' favorite aliens:

In its 78 episodes, "Star Trek" had at least that many species of aliens, mostly humanoid. In some cases, the aliens even resembled characters on other TV series—because it was cheaper to use the other shows' costumes than create new ones. For "A Piece of the Action," featuring a planet of gangsters, they looted the wardrobe from "The Untouchables." For clothing in "Patterns of Force," with its famous Nazi aliens, they raided the ABC series "Combat." Actually, the possiblity that there are other humanoid life forms in the galaxy is remote. But what the heck; it's only TV.

Three of "Trek" 's more memorable aliens:

The Klingons. They're tough. They're mean. They need a shave. In cowboy films of the '30s and '40s, they called these varmints "bad guys." Gene Roddenberry, who had a strong background in TV Westerns, just lifted them out of Dodge City and dropped them into rockets. **Balok**. In "Star Trek" 's tenth episode (actually the third one filmed), the *Enterprise* encounters a giant alien vessel and its huge white commander. Actually, the white guy and his ship are decoys—the real alien, played by Clint "Gentle Ben" Howard, is hiding in a tiny ship, waiting to see if Earth people are really as good as they claim to be.
The Salt Vampire. The last of its kind, it lives on salt—which it sucks out of a human until the person dies. It can take on any appearance, and happens to have picked the form of Nancy Crater, McCoy's old love. It raids the *Enterprise* and kills a few crew members, then becomes extinct.

ALIENS

Uncle Martin strikes a classic pose.

MARTIN THE MARTIAN.
Tim O'Hara, a reporter from the *Los Angeles Sun*, witnessed the crash-landing of a space-ship from Mars. What kind of hideous creature would emerge from the rubble? Some slimy green thing with three eyes and tentacles? No, it was lovable Uncle Martin, played by veteran actor Ray Walston (who'd also done a stint as the devil in *Damn Yankees*). On sitcoms, it turns out, Martians look just like humans—except for the retractable antennae.

THE "DR. WHO" ALIENS.
One expert estimates that there've been 130 to140 different aliens on the show. Here's the most popular species—the Daleks, mechanical warriors who hate anything unlike themselves and are committed to eradicating them. In fact, "exterminate" is their favorite word.

Although they're deadly, they have amusing weaknesses. For example, they move on wheels, so in a typical bit of "Dr. Who" whimsy, they're quite easy to escape; all you do is go upstairs. They can't follow, of course.

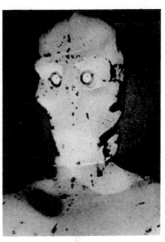

The Andromedan Being.

A CRITIC'S PICK:
David Schow, author of *The Outer Limits: The Official Companion*, picks the four best alien monsters from his favorite sf series:

1. **The "Thetan" from "Architects of Fear."** Robert Culp plays a scientist who tries to unite Earth by transforming himself into an "alien"—"a hideous, scaly, bird-footed, nitrogen-breathing monstrosity"—who will appear at the United Nations General Assembly brandishing a laser pistol,

The Zanti Misfits were created by the same man who gave us Speedy Alka Seltzer.

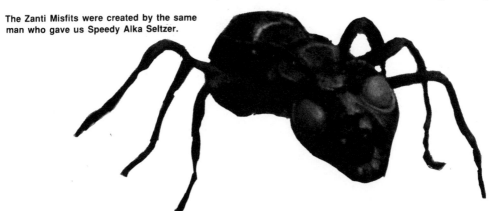

threatening Earth. His hope: all nations will join together to fight a common enemy. But he never makes it—three hunters shoot him near his lab.

Schow: *"There are several ghastly and convincing stages of Robert Culp's alienization, with the coup de grace being an awesome costume worn by stuntman Janos Prohaska in the final act."*

2. The Chromoite from "The Mice."

A being from the planet Chromo is transported to Earth by scientists in an experimental exchange program. The "gelatinous crab-clawed biped" turns out to be Chromo's leading scientist, secretly sent to grow food on Earth for his world. After it murders an Earth scientist, it is shot down.

Schow: *"Astounding in its sheer outrageousness."*

3. The "Box Demon" from "Don't Open Till Doomsday."

In 1929, a gift bearing a card inscribed, "Don't Open Till Doomsday" is delivered to two newlyweds. The groom peers into the box and is instantly transported inside it, where an alien being awaits. The Box Demon will free the man only if he'll help destroy the universe.

Schow: *"Notable not because it is a terrific monster, per se, but because the costume whipped up by Projects Unlimited to serve the allegorical needs of the script was, accordingly, a wild amalgam of phallic and vaginal symbology. The one-eyed beast had a stunted penile head, waving sausage fingers, socketlike vaginal 'gashes' and drooping, pendulous breasts!"*

4. The criminal Zantis from "The Zanti Misfits."

A ship full of criminals from the planet Zanti—"large, ant-like insect[s] about a foot long, with humanoid faces, round-pupilled eyes, and tiny, mean teeth"—arrives on Earth, exiled here by their government. When they attack and kill Bruce Dern, the military steps in and destroys them. The Zantis send a message thanking Earth, explaining that, "We are incapable of executing our own species, but you are not. You are practiced executioners."

Schow: *"Not the greatest, but certainly the most famous among fans of the show. [Special effects man] Wah Chang took particular pains to individually 'characterize' each of the four Zanti models used for the stop-motion animation close-up shots."*

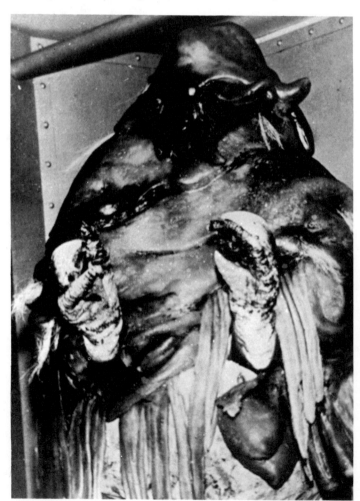

The Chromoite.

The Critics' Choice:
Science Fiction Cult Favorites

IT CAME FROM JAPAN

Old Japanese monsters never die—they just show up on TV. This is actually an old Godzilla suit, slightly altered to create a new, terrifying menace for Ultraman to fight to the death (the monster's, of course).

LOOKING EAST

From the Land of the Rising Sun comes some of the weirdest, tackiest, most absurd and entertaining science fiction television ever created—intended for juvenile audiences in Japan, but admired in America by teenagers and adults. Animation freaks love the clean, stylized, high-tech cartoons. Fans of the live-action programs are simply amazed that the shows exist at all. By American standards, the plots and costuming are so ridiculous that they border on the surreal.

"There'a big Japanese following here," says author/fan Joel Eisner, "particularly for the live action stuff—there are clubs all over the country.

"Of course shows like 'Ultraman' aren't adult-oriented; they're all fantasy programs. But it seems that the more absurd—the more outrageous and ridiculous the characters get—the more the Japanese love them. No matter how preposterous it is, the Japanese will buy it—they'll sit through episode after episode, never questioning why people are running around in chicken suits pretending to be aliens. A lot of the 'Ultraman' villains are just unbelievable—one has a phone head, another has a train head, another has a swimming pool head."

This is a cultural phenomenon that has never really translated.

"Over here," Eisner says, "it's, 'Hey, there's a guy in a rubber suit with a zipper up the back—with a telephone head!' But Japanese kids are willing to suspend disbelief for guys in rubber suits. To them it's far more believable to have a radiation monster that might've come from the War years and mutated than a man-made monster like Frankenstein. Japanese monsters are natural monsters; they come out of volcanoes, or the earth, or the ocean."

Today, monsters have become so popular in Japan that a genre of superhero has emerged just to stop them—the monster-fighter. Using a weird combination of traditional skills (like karate) and science fiction nonsense, heroes like Ultraman take on whatever bizarre creatures the Earth can dish out, protecting the little people of the planet while kids cheer lustily from their living rooms, week after week.

One of the few live-action Japanese series currently available for syndication in the US is "Johnny Sokko and his Flying Robot," about a little boy who uses his high-tech giant to save the Earth every week. (Photo © American International Television, Inc. 1969)

IT CAME FROM JAPAN

ULTRAMAN

TIME: The 21st century.

PLACE: Japan, usually Tokyo.

BACKGROUND: Two giant UFOs collide just outside Earth's atmosphere, and both hurtle towards the planet. One crashes harmlessly into a lake. But the other smashes into a rocket ship piloted by **Iota**, a member of the Science Patrol. Iota is killed instantly.

The enormous alien responsible for his death, a visitor from the Nebula M-78 in the 40th galaxy, feels terrible about the whole incident. To make amends, he not only resurrects Iota, but joins their identities together. "You and I will become one," the alien declares, "and we will fight as one for the peace of Earth for all time to come." Then he gives Iota a Beta Capsule. Whenever **Iota** raises it to the sky he will temporarily become **Ultraman**.

This is a lucky development for Earth, because in the next century our planet will be plagued by a zooful of malevolent monsters. They hatch from eggs, mutate from bacteria cells, grow out of pollution, emerge from active volcanoes. You name it.

THE MISSION: Save Earth from the weekly monster. There *is* an organization equipped to locate and combat the monsters—the **Science Patrol** (Scientific Investigation Agency), located in Tokyo. But even they can't stop the beasts most of the time. No, when **Red King** (a giant pear-shaped alligator) or **Baltan** (a crayfish monster with an asthmatic laugh) begin rampaging through cities, tearing down buildings and stomping on cars, the only one who can save us is **Ultraman**.

SECRETS OF THE SHOW:
The action in "Ultraman" almost always follows a formula:
  1) The monster shows up.
  2) Ultraman shows up.
  3) Ultraman is defeated.
  4) The monster goes on a rampage.
  5) Ultraman returns and beats the monster in hand-to-hand combat. The monster usually explodes in a scene of foam rubber gore.

"It has the same effect on kids over there that pro wrestling has on Americans," muses a fan. "It's two guys in monster suits throwing each other around. The plots are little morality plays—good vs. evil—but really, the stories are secondary. It's the action that grabs people. It's *Godzilla* on a low budget. The more monsters, the better."

Ultraman readies another karate chop for the evil monster, King Joe.

101

A scene from "Johnny Sokko." The plot: In the twenty-first century, aliens arrive on Earth and force a Japanese scientist to build Giant Robot to destroy the planet. Meanwhile, Johnny is shipwrecked on an island that turns out to be the aliens' hideout and laboratory. He's caught and learns that Giant Robot will forever obey the first voice it hears over a remote control device built into a wristwatch. Johnny grabs it and becomes the robot's master. He subsequently uses Giant Robot to defeat the Monster of the Week. Above: Giant Robot takes on a floating eye with tentacles. (Photo © American International Television, Inc. 1969)

THE ULTRAMAN PHENOMENON

From a 1985 Channels *magazine article by Mark Siegel, a professor at Wyoming University who was a visting instructor in Japan at the time.*

Just when the situation seems hopeless, when the blimp-sized blowfish with the porcupine quills and elephant feet is closing in on our main reactor. … Wait! There in the sky! Is it a bird? A plane? Ultraman?

He's enormous but kind of skinny, and he's wearing an almond-eyed plastic mask and a red and silver rubberized jumpsuit. Some Americans may re-member him from the thirty-six episodes that were once syndicated in the United States, but after nineteen seasons on the air in Japan he has transcended the status of mere television star: He's the prototypical hero of an entire genre of quintessentially Japanese action series.

This good guy has saved society more times than any other superhero flying the earth's airwaves. And he's done it with nary a plot twist nor audience-winning wisecrack. In Ultraman's world the characters and action are straightforward. A monster is threatening Earth—Zazarn, King Joe, Gorgon, or some other recombinant creature from legends and zoos, gorgeous in concept but more like gorged Goodyear in execution. Down come Ultraman's big aluminum-foil feet, and, after a double order of double takes, the two behemoths join in a fight scene as ritualized as a High Mass.

But "Ultraman," its sequels, and its imitators are much more than martial arts fantasies. To the Japanese they're reassuring rituals deeply rooted in the nation's history, hopes, and fears. The key to Ultraman lies in the society's profoundly mixed feelings about things foreign.

IT CAME FROM JAPAN

For almost 2,000 years the Japanese have been the greatest cultural borrowers in the world. At the same time, they remain a unique and tradition-oriented society, adapting outside influences to fit their culture and discarding what doesn't seem beneficial.

But in the past century and a half, the Japanese have been shocked into an awareness of their extreme vulnerability to outside forces. Consider: Japan awoke one day in 1853—after two centuries of almost complete isolation under the Tokugowa shoguns—to find Commodore Perry parking about a third of the American Navy in Tokyo Bay. Forced to open their ports and accept a series of colonial tariffs, Japan began to thrive by adapting Western industrialization to her own culture.

At the same time, the densely populated country, lacking in natural resources, came to rely heavily on trade. Thus, when the West's great depression arrived in the 1930s, Japan believed herself virtually forced into World War II in a hunt for new markets and resources. Even today the Japanese tend to associate their guilt over the war with the notion that military aggression is the wrong way to expand one's economy. In the midst of their stupendous postwar recovery, the Japanese were again reminded of their dependence and vulnerability: The Arab oil embargo of the 1970s temporarily gave them the world's highest inflation rate.

"Ultraman" borrows from this history a number of elements that have particular resonance for the Japanese. Earth faces inevitable attack by the evil monstrosities that populate various alien worlds. To defend the planet, the benevolent Ultra family comes from a distant nebula and builds a major base in Japan, manned by 300 scientists and monster-fighters as well as a number of elite assistants to Ultraman.

The hero himself gives up his own off-duty life to assume the identity of Iota, a Japanese family man whom he accidentally killed. When crisis comes, Iota changes into the giant in the rubberized jumpsuit to do battle with monsters who can be defeated only by someone possessing similar size and power—and an equally hilarious and cheap costume. Just as the Japanese responded to the oddly dressed barbarians brought in by Commodore Perry, Ultraman adopts the invaders' size and technology.

Ultraman is not quite human or monster or machine, but a union, an android. Likewise, his fighting style is partly traditional Japanese and partly technological hocus-pocus. He doesn't fear the monsters' strength. The Japanese admire strength and almost always seek to turn it to their advantage through kind of cultural jujitsu.

Iota is in many ways typical of the Japanese businessman who comes home from his high-tech work, shrugs off his blue business suit, and sits down on the tatami to a cup of green tea and a plate of sashimi. Society is presented as healthy and stable in "Ultraman" and nearly every one of its dozens of spinoffs. The threat comes from inhuman forces, or forces seen to be of outside origin, such as modern technology. When Ultraman defeats the monster of the week, society is not advanced, improved, or moved in some new direction—it is returned to its original state. Despite enormous progress and change over the last 150 years, the Japanese tend to see their society as continuing in the proud tradition of two millennia, and to see the alien intruders as bizarre and powerful, offering opportunity but threatening disruption and cultural devastation.

When the plot doesn't involve attacks on mankind, it often concerns the alien monsters' never-ending wars of aggression against one another. Several monsters face off, threatening to destroy Japan. The pattern reflects what the Japanese think of as their "demilitarized" position in the world: They see themselves as peace-loving pawns of the superpowers' machinations.

Villains in "Ultraman" and its spinoffs are usually trying to weaken, corrupt, and eventually overthrow Japanese society. While the villains sometimes attack the island by causing tidal waves and other traditional Japanese disasters, they just as often attempt to subvert the society's morals. In one favorite plot of "Uchu Keiji Shiaraiban" (Space Policeman Shiaraiban), the villains hypnotize young brides who then forsake the marriages honorably proposed by their parents in order to unwittingly wed some alien demon. But there is worse in store for the traditional, peace-loving island dwellers, as the monsters brainwash houswives into abandoning homemaking responsibilities in misguided pursuit of jazzercise classes. The space policeman's work is never done.

ASTROBOY

TIME: The year 2000.

PLACE: An unspecified Earth city.

BACKGROUND: A young boy named Astor Boynton III is killed in a car accident, and his distraught father—a brilliant scientist who heads the Institute of Science—decides to memorialize him by building a robot duplicate.

In fact, Dr. Boynton attempts to *improve* on his son. He gives the robot superstrength and installs rockets in each of his legs, enabling him to fly (the feet just sort of drop out of sight and flames shoot out the bottoms of his legs). Boynton christens his new "son" Astroboy.

Unfortunately, the scientist flips out while he's working on the project. He creates Astroboy in the image of an eight- or nine-year-old, then goes crazy (literally) trying to figure out why Astroboy doesn't get any older. Eventually, Dr. Boynton begins to hate Astroboy, and spitefully sells him to a robot circus.

While Astroboy toils unhappily in the circus, Dr. Boynton is replaced at the Institute of Science by Dr. Pachedyrmus Elefon, a compassionate man with an enormous nose. Dr. Elefon is an activist for robots' rights, and tries to free Astroboy. The circus owner refuses, but it's a moot point; while they're arguing, the government passes a law liberating all robots. Astroboy goes to live with Dr. Elefon at the Institute of Science. And whenever there's a mad scientist, monster, or supercrook on the loose, Astroboy flies to the scene.

OTHER CHARACTERS:
- **Astro-parents**: When Astroboy wishes for a real family, Elefon builds a few robots to keep him company. The "parents" are never major characters; they're around to tuck Astroboy into bed at night, and make him feel loved.
- **Astrogirl**: Astroboy's earthbound robot sister, who has no superpowers other than the invulnerability of her robot body. She frequently gets into tomboyish mischief, then Astroboy has to rescue her.
- **Mr. Pompous**: An old bald man with a droopy mustache, a rough but friendly private investigator who looks like Wimpy on "Popeye."

- **The Villains**: Mostly one-shot characters, like **I.Q. Plenty**, a mad scientist who threatens to destroy every robot in the world (including Astroboy) and **Freddie Fink,** a mafia-type, cold-blooded killer .

CRITIC'S COMMENTS: "In some respects, Astroboy was like Pinnochio, the puppet who wanted to be a real boy. One episode, for example, began with him and a bunch of friends watching a horror movie. The children were frightened by the ghosts and monsters—but Astroboy couldn't work up any emotion. He began to fret that despite his strength and his ability to fly, he wasn't as good as a real person because he couldn't feel. In fact, he got so disconsolate about it that Dr. Elefon finally agreed to program fear into him.

"After one episode, he was glad to get rid of the fear. But he insisted that the experience was rewarding because it made him feel like a real human."

In 1963, "Astroboy" became the first Japanese cartoon series ever exported to America. It was originally a half-hour black-and-white cartoon show, with one hundred four episodes. But the character was so popular that in the '80s a new animated series—in color this time—was produced and released.

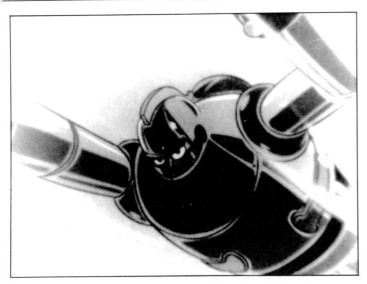

Gigantor attacks. Of the ninety-six "Gigantor" episodes that were filmed, only fifty-six made it to America in 1966.

GIGANTOR

TIME: The year 2000.

PLACE: Earth, in an unspecified city. When the action takes place in Japan, they say, "Gigantor has just arrived in Japan."

BACKGROUND: Gigantor's real name is Iron Man 28. It was originally a secret weapon designed by the Japanese during World War II to aid the Nazis. But it was never perfected.

When the Japanese lost the war, their government lost interest in the project. But it became an obsession with Professor Sparks, the scientist working on it. He built super-robot after super-robot, trying to get one right. And finally, with the twenty-eighth model, he succeeded. He created a 30-foot-tall, indestructible mechanical man that had no voice or brain of its own. It was controlled by anyone who carried a special hand-held remote device.

Of course, the US and Japan were at peace by this time, so Iron Man 28 was used to fight crime instead of Americans. [Later, when the program was westernized, he became Gigantor, a classic good-guy robot. The original pilot film was never aired in the US, due to the World War II theme.]

THE CHARACTERS: Professor Sparks died soon after his robot was created, so ownership—and control—of Gigantor was passed on to his son, Jimmy.
•**Jimmy Sparks**: A rather unusual 12-year-old boy: he lives in a house all by himself; he never goes to school; he drives a car, carries a gun, and works with the police department; and he wears only shorts.
•**Dr. Bob Brilliant**: a scientist.
•**Buttons**: His son, a friend of Jimmy's.
•**Secret Agent Dick Strong**: Infiltrator of criminal organizations.
•**Chief Inspector Blooper:** The comic relief. Wears a little mustache and an oversized uniform.

THE VILLAINS: There are no petty crooks in this show—they all want to take over the world, either by using a secret weapon, or by stealing Gigantor. A few examples:
•**Professor Stringer**: Invents a giant robot called Big Fang, a takeoff on the old Aurora Frankenstein model kit. In Japan he's called Frankenstein Ug-A-Blob.
•**Mr. Lurk**: Steals the blueprints to Gigantor, and along with Professor Tic Tac Toe, builds a duplicate of him.
•**Mr. Double-Trouble**: Owns the smoke robots, which transform themselves into smoke.
•**The Space Pussies**: Alien cats from the Planet Pussywillow. They attack Gigantor with a robot named Magnaman.

CRITIC'S COMMENTS: "I don't really know why people like the animation. It's really very primitive. In fact, people used to make fun of Gigantor himself. They called him 'The Flying Water Tank,' 'Old Needle-Nose,' and various things like that. The audience identification was really with the little kid, who had this tremendous weapon—a sort of cross between a knight in armor and a giant robot—and it was all at his personal control."
—**Fred Patten,**
Animation Historian

EIGHTH MAN

TIME: 21st century.

PLACE: Metro City.

BACKGROUND: Detective Peter Brady of Metro International Police is murdered by the arch-villain Saucer Lip. Luckily Dr. Genius, a brilliant scientist who looks like a cross between Captain Kangaroo and Cesar Romero, happens to be passing by at the time. He takes the dying police officer to his lab, where he's been working on a superandroid, and prepares to transplant Brady's life force into the robot's body.

Dr. Genius has tried this experiment seven times before and failed in every attempt. But this time it works, and Brady—the eighth man—is saved.

THE EIGHTH MAN: Brady still looks normal, but as an android, he now has superpowers; he possesses extraordinary strength, can run at lightning speed, and can change his appearance, chameleon-like, to look like anyone he wishes. But despite his new abilities, he doesn't feel superior; in fact, he immediately begins agonizing that he's not as good as he used to be, because now he's just an android. What, for example, will his girlfriend think?

THE MISSION: Regardless, Brady is committed to carrying on the fight against crime. He changes his name to Tobor (robot spelled backwards) and sets up the Tobor Detective Agency. Most of Tobor's foes work for Intercrime, an international crime organization with its own island. These include: **Saucer Lip**, the world's most wanted criminal; **Dr. Sinister**, Intercrime's resident genius, inventor of weapons like **Pounce**, the robot tiger; and **Dr. Goldshrinker**, inventor of a gun that changes the molecular structure of gold.

CRITIC'S COMMENTS:
"'Eighth Man' is popular in reputation more than anything else—not many people have actually seen it. But among those who have, its popularity is probably due to the fact it's closer to American comic superheroes than most Japanese programs. In fact, 'Eighth Man' is somewhat similar to the old 1940s comic hero 'Spectre.'

"It's also, let's say, more honestly violent than standard American cartoons. If Tobor punches somebody, the character is obviously going to the hospital—if not the grave—with a broken skull. In American cartoons, you can have frantic slugfests and nobody even needs a bandage."

—**Fred Patten,**
Animation Historian

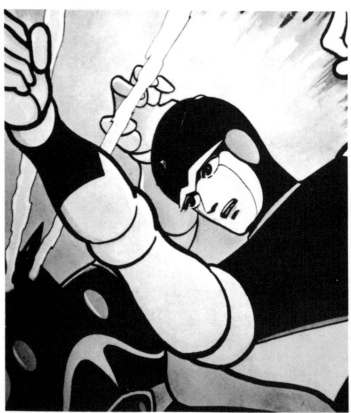

"Eighth Man" arrived in America in 1965, with fifty-two syndicated episodes.

IT CAME FROM JAPAN

ROBOTECH

"Robotech" is the *Lord of the Rings* of imported Japanese animation—an epic trilogy that includes eighty-five episodes and spans forty years. The plot is extremely complicated, with an enormous cast of characters—and its theme is unusually somber for a TV cartoon: Earth is attacked by various alien invaders, and as the final episode ends, what's left of the human race is enslaved by crablike creatures called Invids. Only a small resistance movement and the hoped-for return of an Earth battle fleet offer hope.

"The original Japanese series was called 'Macross.' It was a very tightly written, serialized TV novel that ran for thirty-six episodes. The American company that wanted to bring it over here and sell it to the syndicated market got hung up by the problem that American TV buyers weren't interested in anything less than sixty-five episodes in the syndication package. And there weren't any good Japanese programs that they could find with that many episodes. So what they did was buy three programs that they felt were similar enough to allow them, with clever writing, to claim that this was the same show taking place over three generations."
—**Fred Patten,**
Animation Historian

PART I: THE MACROSS SAGA

TIME: A.D. 2009

PLACE: Our solar system.

BACKGROUND: In the year 1999, a gigantic space battleship crash-lands on Earth. There is a global civil war going on at the time, but the implication that a race advanced enough to have created this battlefortress exists is enough to convince Earth's governments to stop fighting and pool their resources to defend themselves. They put the world's best minds to work on trying to get inside the ship and learning to use it. Soon an entire community, numbering some 70,000 people, springs up in the vicinity of the spaceship, supporting the task.

THE PLOT: Ten years later, humans finally master the fundamental operations of the ship. But just as Captain Gloval and his crew are getting ready to take it on its maiden voyage, giant mercenaries sent by the original aliens who built it—sixty-foot-tall humanoids called Zentraedi—show up to reclaim their masters' property. Fighting breaks out between Earth and the aliens.

Captain Gloval attempts lift-off. But he accidentally activates a control that puts a sort of force-field around both the ship and the scientific community, warping the whole thing out to the orbit of Pluto. Worse, the hyperspace device that takes them there burns out immediately; so they have to fly all the way back from Pluto to Earth under normal rocket power—which takes two years.

During this time there are battles with the aliens, and all kinds of soap-opera-ish developments among various members of the cast—most of whom are young. For example:

• A main character, fighter pilot Roy Fokker, is injured in battle and dies at his girlfriend Claudia's apartment. His best friend, teenage pilot Rick Hunter, then becomes the primary hero.
• Meanwhile, Hunter falls for Lynn Minmei, who aspires to be

Rick Hunter, a teenager who becomes the hero of the "Macross Saga," in battle with the alien invader. (Photo © Harmony Gold, 1985)

a movie star. He also saves Lisa Hayes, a pretty officer who is falling in love with him— although he is unaware of it.

• Max Sterling, one of the pilots in Hunter's unit, incurs the wrath of Miriya, Zentraedi ace pilot, by besting her in battle. She shrinks herself to his size so she can confront him in person and kill him. But he wins again and they get married instead, and have the first interspecies baby, Dana Sterling.

• Lynn Minmei becomes a movie star, the most popular girl in town, and a singing sensation. The Zentraedi, who have never heard music, think she is a secret weapon. Rick worries that he's lost her to her cousin Kyle, who proposes to her at the hospital. But does Rick really love her or Lisa? Will she marry Kyle? Stay tuned.

Eventually, a select group of the Zentraedi and the humans in space join forces; but it's too late to save Earth. Directing the war from their home planet, the supreme commander of the Zentraedi sends an army of more than four million ships to wipe out humanity once and for all. In desperation, Captain Gloval rams the invaders' lead ship head-on, miraculously causing a huge explosion that destroys the marauding force— but also devastates Earth. The battle isn't over yet, though. The Zentraedi are trained to fight, and peaceful coexistence with humans begins to bore them. They join forces with a renegade Zentraedi commander and attack Earth again. This time they're defeated, but the battleship and most of humanity are destroyed along with them. As the first segment ends, Rick Hunter and his true love,

Lisa Hayes, stare at the empty skies, ready to repopulate Earth.

PART II: THE ROBOTECH MASTERS

"The lead character in Part II was a teenage girl and a military cadet, supposedly Max and Miriya's daughter, Dana. In the 'Macross Saga,' since she was supposed to be an alien baby, they showed her with green hair. But when Harmony Gold brought in the second TV series, saying this was the same girl grown up, she was a blonde. They got a lot of viewers writing in saying, 'How come her hair changed color?' "

—Fred Patten

TIME: A.D. 2024

PLACE: Earth.

BACKGROUND: The story begins to get very complicated here. The Zentraedi, it turns out, are biogenetically engi-

Dana Sterling, Earth's first interspecies inhabitant. (Photo © Harmony Gold, 1985)

neered clones employed by members of an intergalactic police force created eons ago by advanced human beings—a sort of scientific elite—called Robotech Masters. The Robotech Empire has begun to degenerate and the Masters need something called Protoculture to keep body and soul together. The secret of its creation lies in the wreck of their flagship, which crashed on Earth at the beginning of the series. It's still somewhere on the planet, and the Robotech Masters need to have it back.

Since the Zentraedi were defeated in the first part of the series, the Robotech Masters decide to come to Earth and personally finish wiping out the humans.

THE PLOT: After Part I's holocaust destroys civilization, a hardy breed of humans rebuilds society and develops a military academy to train soldiers to defend New Earth against future space villains. As Part II opens, cadet Dana Sterling, the interspecies baby born to Max and Miriya in Part I, is graduating.

Just then, the Robotech Masters attack; Dana is established as the show's hero when her squadron saves the planet.

A devastating war between Earth and the Robotech Masters ensues, with neither side giving an inch. But the Robotech Masters fight on two fronts: on the battlefield, and with spies. They attempt to infiltrate the humans with bioengineered clones who are brain-treated to believe that they are really human. After they work their way into the human society and get hired in positions of trust, Robotech Masters activate their brain control and make them betray the government.

Dana becomes romantically involved with a particularly handsome spy named Zor—actually the clone of the man who developed Robotechnology and subsequently invented the Zentraedi and Protoculture. The Robotech Masters had hoped he could reinvent the stuff for them, but he can't. Dana realizes what he is and wonders whether he can be cured—another soap opera-ish subplot. And in fact, he does escape his masters'control. Then he returns to the Robotech ship and destroys them—along with most of Earth.

The segment ends with just about everybody killing one another off. The main character doesn't die, exactly, but it's obvious that both Earth and the Robotech Masters have pretty much exhausted their resources fighting each other—which is too bad, because another invader is on the way.

PART III: THE NEW GENERATION

TIME: A.D. 2069

PLACE: Earth.

BACKGROUND: At the end of the original "Macross" series, it is explained that Rick Hunter and his group have built a spaceship of their own and have gone off into space looking for the home planet of the mysterious Robotech Masters—not realizing that the Robotech Masters are already mounting an attack on Earth. So in Part III, the main hero is a young member of the succeeding generation of the space armada.

THE PLOT: In the wake of the

Rand, Annie, and Scott Bernard in "Robotech." (Photo © Harmony Gold, 1985)

second round of Robotech wars, a new enemy arrives and conquers Earth—the Invid, a crablike parasitic species that apparently thrives on Protoculture. Earth is reduced to an Invid slave colony, where humanity exists to "harvest and process Protoculture." A contingent from Admiral Rick Hunter's fleet returns to Earth to save man, but gets wiped out by the Invid; the only survivor is Lt. Scott Bernard. Through the course of this third segment, he rallies other young humans around him and they start an underground guerrilla movement. They manage to destroy one Invid base, and the series ends with Scott Bernard giving an uplifting speech, something to the effect of, "Just as we destroyed this one base, we're gonna go and wipe out the rest of their bases, and any day now we're expecting Admiral Hunter to return with the rest of the Earth Fleet, and we'll wipe them out and be a happy planet once

again." And that's it.

"'Robotech' 's creator, Carl Macek, says that one of the really frustrating things about marketing the series is that TV programmers don't realize it was designed to appeal to the 'Star Trek' audience. His company has told every TV market they've sold the show to that if they put it on in the same timeslot as 'Star Trek' reruns, it's going to pick up a big audience. But instead, most stations put it in the general kiddie cartoon hour. Of course, little kids aren't sophisticated enough to understand it, and most kids can't handle a saga that goes on this long anyway.

"So...the main complaints against the series—that it'stoo hard for kids to understand, that there's too much violence in it, and that it's controversial—aren't particularly valid. It's supposed to be geared to teenagers and adults, not children."
—Fred Patten

BRITISH INVASION

British programs have always attracted cult followings in America, but in prime time, their ratings have been disappointing. That's because their approach to TV is different than America's.

British TV companies don't have enormous sums of money to spend on sets, special effects, or props. They can't afford to blow up planes or destroy cars just to entertain their viewers—so they have to rely on imaginative plot lines and character development instead. American audiences clearly prefer lots of slam-bang action. But good characters are the essence of cult appeal.

"Here's where I think British TV wins out," explains critic John Peel, a native of England. "The special effects may be weak, but the stories are better. The British give you more character; they're interested in motivation—'Why are people doing these things?' as opposed to, 'Here's the monster of the week, let's kill it dead'—which is the way American TV tends to work."

Better-known British sf shows, like "Dr. Who," are listed among the best (or worst) programs in this book. But there are others, known to only a few devoted American fans, that also deserve recognition.

Briton David McCallum starred in two science fiction programs after "The Man From UNCLE" was canceled in 1968. In 1975, he played the title role in an American remake of "The Invisible Man"—a fiasco that lasted only four months and thirteen episodes. Then in 1981 he starred in "Sapphire and Steel."

SAPPHIRE & STEEL

TIME: Based in the present, but the characters never stay there. Since the theme is time travel, it could be any time, any place, anywhere.

PLACE: Generally, Earth. Also strange places that they never identify—probably other dimensions, but who knows?

BACKGROUND: Start by throwing out all your ideas about what is and isn't logical. Imagine that time is like a tunnel. The sixteenth century, for example, is one part of the tunnel, the twentieth century another. Outside the tunnel are the forces of chaos and destruction, which are always trying to get into our universe or dimension; Sapphire and Steel's mission is to stop them. Whenever a negative force breaks through the time barriers, Sapphire and Steel are dispatched to force them back.

We never know who's sending them, or where they come from. All we know is that something, somewhere, has selected Sapphire and Steel for their mission.

HEROES:
•**Steel** (David McCallum): Has gray eyes and always wears gray. He is an antihero—tough, totally unemotional, totally amoral. And he'll do anything that needs to be done. "When he smiles," says a fan, "you know he's going to do something dirty." His powers vary as he needs them, but they're based on the attributes of steel. He has enormous strength, possesses the power to withstand the flow of time, and can reduce his body to subzero temperatures. He's extremely opinionated, with a very analytical mind. We don't know what he really looks like; he just appears human

BRITISH SF

Joanna Lumley's second cult series, "Sapphire and Steel" (her first was "The New Avengers"), aired in England in 1980 and 1981. There were fourteen episodes in the first season and eighteen in the second. In the final episode, the heroes were imprisoned somewhere "outside time"—for no apparent reason—by their own people. No sequel is expected.

combines sex, gentleness, and strength; everyone falls in love with her—except Steel, who doesn't love anything. In fact, Steel's personality infuriates her. Her powers include the ability to see through time and reverse it for a short period. She can also hold an object and tell its history. Perfect talents for an investigator.

•**Silver** (David Collings): A gadget man, he is an electrical genius who makes occasional appearances whenever S. & S. need something built. A little effeminate, sybaritic. Sapphire loves him, but Steel thinks he's a wimp and can't stand him.

VILLAINS:

They're not people—just forces: chaos, anarchy, hate, destruction. If they break through the time barrier, the universe will start falling apart because they're breaking up the order of things. Manifest themselves as glowing balls of light, or humans with no faces. They can always be defeated, but they're very powerful and the longer they stay in our dimension, the stronger they become.

while he's on earth—a disguise he's not very fond of.
•**Sapphire** (Joanna Lumley): Has bright blue eyes and always dresses in blue. She's assigned as Steel's partner to keep him from destroying everything in sight. An ideal woman who

Bombs away. A little-known science fiction clunker is the 1977 British/Australian production, "Star Maidens." The plot: The planet Medusa, where women rule and men are menials, drifts into our Solar System. Two Medusan men escape their world via flying saucer and crash on Earth. To them, our world is a paradise, because men "rule" and women handle most of the drudgery, but the Star Maidens, Medusan rulers, want the men back and head to Earth to capture them. Episodes center around the inevitably weird interaction between Earth and Medusan societies.

THE INVISIBLE MAN

TIME: The late 1950s.

PLACE: Britain, an old country house just outside London.

BACKGROUND: Dr. Peter Brady, a British scientist, was experimenting with an invisibility serum—using himself as a guinea pig—when he accidentally took an overdose and turned completely invisible. He doesn't know how to reverse the process. So he's stuck. He's the Invisible Man.

Brady's face is never actually seen by the audience. When he is visible at all, he's wrapped in bandages. The rest of the time, his presence is indicated by adroit special effects: a wineglass being raised to an unseen mouth, a door opening and shutting, a cigarette floating in midair, being puffed. ("I still haven't figured out how they did that one," says an expert, "and it was filmed thirty years ago.")

Although the series was inspired by the famous H.G. Wells story, Brady isn't anything like Wells's crazed character (who became obsessed with power and began murdering people). Brady is a regular guy; a good-natured, civic-minded Briton who just happens to be invisible. He isn't terribly brilliant. He isn't even incognito. And since everyone knows about his affliction, he is approached each week by people who want his assistance. Sometimes he helps out friends, sometimes he works with the police taking on terrorists, crooks, crazy scientists, etc. And occasionally he does government work because a friend of his works for "The Ministry." But his main goal in life is to become visible again. The series ends before he does.

CRITIC'S COMMENT: " 'The Invisible Man' still turns up occasionally in syndication, but most people will still never see it—which is too bad. The plots may be a little corny, but it's got a good feel to it—a nice, crisp b&w texture—and some of the special effects work is superb. Definitely an underrated gem."
—**John Peel,**
Files **Magazine**

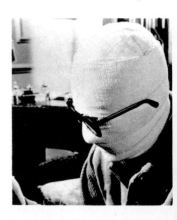

Thirteen episodes of "The Invisible Man" aired on CBS in America from November 4, 1958, to January 27, 1959. Then it disappeared.

UFO

TIME: The end of the 20th century.

PLACE: Earth and environs. Sometimes the moon, where man has established a small colony called Moon Base, sometimes outer space; usually Earth.

BACKGROUND: As the year 2000 approaches, the human race faces its greatest threat: Unidentified aliens are invading Earth in pyramid-shaped UFOs. Their race is sterile and cannot reproduce; the only way they can stay alive is with organ transplants. To acquire spare body parts, they kidnap human beings, haul them back to their planet, and dismember them. Earth's only defense against these space barbarians is SHADO—Supreme Headquarters, Alien Defense Organization—an international organization with the mandate and technology to fight alien invasions. Its headquarters, an underground bunker stocked with futuristic machinery and the controls for incredible array of firepower and gadgetry, is hidden beneath a film studio just outside London.

SHADO fights aliens three ways: First, there's SID (Space Intruder Detector), a satellite that registers UFOs when they get near Earth; it alerts Moon Base, whose interceptors are Earth's first line of defense. The second is *Skydiver*, a combination supersub/aircraft which attacks the UFOs in flight if they get past the moon base and enter Earth's atmosphere. And the third, employed if the UFOs happen to land, is the tanklike SHADO-mobile, which can be air-dropped into place. Each of these high-tech weapons is used only if the preceding one fails.

SHADO is an effective paramilitary force, but Earth is in big trouble; we can't really stop the aliens until they figure out where the invaders are coming from … and thus far, that's a mystery. In the meantime, hang on to your arms and legs.

MAIN CAST:
• **Ed Straker** (Ed Bishop): Head of SHADO. An abrasive, take-charge guy who'll do anything it takes to accomplish his goals.
• **Col. Alec Freeman** (George Sewell): SHADO's second-in-command. Amiable, efficient,

Greetings from Moon Base. "UFO" was the first live-action TV series for Gerry Anderson, creator of supermarionation. It was syndicated in America in 1972; there were twenty-six episodes. (Photo courtesy ITC Entertainment, Inc.)

conciliatory. Smooths over unpleasant situations created by Strker's abrasiveness. A field man.
• **Lt. Gay Ellis** (Gabrille Drake): In charge of Moon Base; young, pretty, has purple hair (all the women on the moon base wear purple wigs). She's the sex symbol of the show, and to prove it, she does a semi-strip in the first episode.
• **Capt. Peter Karlin** (Peter Gordeno, a popular English singer): Captain of *Skydiver*. Introverted, moody but efficient. Out to avenge his sister, who was killed by the aliens.
• **Col. Paul Foster** (Michael Billington): Another sex symbol. Action man who shoots up the aliens—mows them down with machine guns, revolvers, anything he has at hand.
• **The Aliens:** Green-hued people who wear big, bulky spacesuits and breathe a thick, viscous water (without which they die). They're seen a few times, but little is revealed about them.

BLAKE'S 7

HISTORY: In 1985, "Blake's 7" was an obscure English science fiction TV series. A year and a half later, it had become the hottest underground cult show in America.

The reason for its sudden emergence was simple: eight years after it premiered in England, "Blake's 7" finally made it onto American television. In the fall of 1986, several PBS stations aired "the British 'Star Trek' " for the first time. Predictably, sf fans went wild.

"I would like you to know," one viewer wrote to Philadelphia TV station WHYY, "that ... I have never been as engrossed by any show." Another wrote: "Thank you, thank you, thank you. 'Blake's 7' is the best science fiction series I have ever seen."

"Blake's 7" was just as well received in Britain, where it aired from 1978 to 1981. By its fourth and final season, there were at least ten English fan clubs for the show—as well as a *Blake's 7* magazine that sold 40,000 copies every month. Its final episode was watched by 10 million people in Britain—making it "Dr. Who" 's rival as the most popular British science fiction show of its time. It was also broadcast in thirty-one foreign countries.

ORIGIN: "Blake's 7" was created by Terry Nation, a prolific scriptwriter whose credits include work on "The Baron," "The Champions," "The Persuaders," "The Saint," "The Avengers," and "Dr. Who." In fact, Nation is the man who invented the Daleks for "Dr. Who."

One day in the mid-'70s, Nation met with BBC exceceutives to discuss new television projects. Although the network was eager to find a vehicle for his talents, they couldn't seem to come up with anything. Nation became desperate. "This is mistakenly called a 'flash of inspiration,' " he says. "The interview was drawing to a close when I surprised myself by starting to detail a new science fiction adventure. ... 'Have you got a title?' someone asked. 'Blake's 7,' I replied without hesitation. When I left the BBC that day, I had a commission to write a pilot script and the bewildered feeling that once again I could not trace the source of the idea."

One of the sources was clearly "Star Trek." Another was *Star Wars*, whose Imperial Empire probably inspired "Blake's" Federation. But "Blake's 7" isn't just a clone of another show (not the way "Battlestar Galactica" is, anyway). Nation borrowed plot devices, but gave the show a generally unique character by infusing it with his personal ideology. "['Blake's 7'] is not just people tearing around in spaceships, although that might be what it appears," he told Britain's *Starburst* magazine. Instead, the struggle between the Federation and Blake represented a kind of Holy War; to Nation, The Federation embodied the cold-blooded expediency of the Christian knights of the Third Crusade, who actually slaughtered a Christian community in order to earn money to "get the boats to wipe out the heathen community." Despite their pretensions, "They had no regard for Man; they had regard only for the mechanics of Man."

BRITISH SF

Jan Chappell played Cally, the alien devoted to Blake. In the story, she was killed at the beginning of the fourth season, highlighting an unusual feature of the show—many of the main characters were killed off during its run. Blake, for example, was shot by Avon in the final episode; Gan was wiped out in the second season; and even Blake's nemesis, Travis, bit the dust before the third season. (Photo © Scorpio)

The character Blake represents the antithesis of their hypocrisy. "Finally," Nation declared, "somebody has to be on the line that says, 'I at least, am [truly] honorable and I believe in my honor.'"

Nation wrote the entire first season of "Blake's 7," and nineteen scripts in all. But his vision of Blake as a symbol of "honor" was altered toward the end of the show's second season. Story editor Chris Boucher began experimenting with the lead character's personality. "[I was] trying to show the problem of a lot of revolutionary leaders, from Zapata on down. In sustaining that sort of pressure they are inevitably changed," he explains.

THE CULT FOLLOWING: To a lot of fans, Boucher's alterations might symbolize the real beginning of "Blake's 7"—because at this point the characters began emerging from Nation's original outline and developing personalities and relationships on their own. And it is precisely the humanity of the characters that has attracted a hard-core cult following to "Blake's 7." "The most striking features of the show," explains one of America's truly committed fans, "are the relationships between the characters, both the heroes and the villains. They are not cardboard stereotypes."

So if the show succeeds, it's because the players' "private wars" are as interesting to viewers as their war against the Federation. Nothing is static in "Blake's 7." Main characters are killed; personalities change; heroes lose. Nor is there a constant affirmation of the nobility of the human spirit, as there is in "Star Trek." Heroic deeds are performed reluctantly, usually because there is no alternative. In "Blake's 7," people still behave like the human horde we know so well, whether they're floating around in space or safe on the ground.

Paul Darrow (below) was a cult hero here before "Blake's 7" had ever been shown in the US. In fact, the "Blake's 7" phenomenon surprised everyone—even the show's distributor, Lionheart TV. "I just don't understand where they saw the show to begin with," marveled one Lionheart executive during an interview in 1985. (Photo © Paul Darrow)

CULT FAVORITES

Michael Keating, who plays Vila, is another favorite with "Blake's 7" fans. (Photo © Michael Keating)

TIME: The 3rd century of the second calendar.

PLACE: Outer space.

BACKGROUND: "After the chaos of the intergalactic wars, a powerful [intergalactic] government [known as the Federation arose] ... and engulfed most of the populated worlds [of the galaxy]. Liberty became a crime punishable by death ... the majority of the population lived in a state of drug-induced docility.

"Each world had its share of rebels who turned to either crime or the resistance. Through corruption and payoffs, the larger criminal organizations were allowed to exist because they posed no real threat to the Federation. [But] the resistance movement, which was unorganized and composed of small, persistent groups, constituted enough of a threat to warrant termination if caught." One of those rebels, Roj Blake, was arrested on a trumped-up charge and sentenced to exile on the prison colony of Cygnus Alpha. En route, however, he and his fellow prisoners—all legitimate criminals—escaped in an abandoned alien spaceship called the *Liberator* and become the legendary band of rebels known as Blake's 7.

MISSION: To survive by eluding the forces of the Federation; to wreak as much havoc on the Federation's outposts as possible; to overthrow the Federation altogether.

HEROES:
•**Roj Blake** (Garreth Thomas): The Robin Hood of his time, a brilliant outlaw who repeatedly outwits and harasses the authorities. "His name has become the symbol of hope and freedom against oppression throughout the entire resistance movement." Disappears at the end of the second series, a plot twist that coincides with Garreth Thomas's decision to join a Shakespearean acting troupe.
•**Kerr Avon** (Paul Darrow): A cold, unsentimental computer expert. "A genius at self-preservation and completely self-centered." Rarely smiles. "I limit Avon to one smile per episode," Darrow says. Becomes the leader after Blake disappears. By far the show's most popular character.
•**Jenna Stannis** (Sally Knyvette): A smuggler and staunch supporter of Blake.
•**Vila Restal** (Michael Keating): A cowardly thief, more likely to faint in the face of danger than do anything useful. Blake's safecracker.
•**Cally** (Jan Chappell): The resident alien, a "telepathic native of the planet Auron." Trained in guerrilla warfare.
•**Gan Olag** (David Jackson): A man-mountain with an electronic "limitator" implanted in his brain, which prevents him from killing. Ironically, he's the first member of the crew to be killed.
•**Zen** (Peter Tuddenham): Master computer of the *Liberator*, last of the original Blake's 7.
•**Capt. Del Tarrant** (Steven Pacey): Smuggler and mercenary who poses as a Federation officer until joining forces with Avon and the *Liberator*'s crew in the third season.
•**Dayna Mellanby** (Josette Simon): A weapons expert whose family is wiped out by the Federation. Bent on revenge, she joins forces with Avon and company in the third season.

•**Soolin** (Glynis Barber): Beautiful but deadly, a crack shot who joins the crew after Cally is killed. Her private mission: to avenge the death of her parents.

VILLAINS:

•**Federation Supreme Commander Servalan** (Jacqueline Pearce): A cold-blooded female villain. "She is ambitious, amoral, vicious, and capable of killing with her own hands to get what she wants." And what she wants is to rid herself of Blake.

•**Space Commander Travis** (Steven Grief/Brian Croucher): Servalan's "chief butcher," a man who hates Blake so much that he's willing to sell out the entire human race to get him. Even after the Federation strips him of his duties, he pursues Blake fanatically across the galaxy. Avon finally stops him.

Last but not least: John Steed and Emma Peel of "The Avengers."

THE AVENGERS

No list of British science fiction programs would be complete without "The Avengers," a mid-'60s spy spoof that employed some of the wackiest inventions (and inventors) in TV history. Patrick Macnee was paired with four different female partners in his stint as a secret agent: Honor Blackman, Diana Rigg, Linda Thorson, and Joanna Lumley. But most fans agree that Rigg, as Mrs. Emma Peel, was the best.

As for the science fiction: In practically every episode a mad scientist concocted a brilliant scheme to extort millions or threaten the safety of the world (or at least England). In one episode, for example, Frank N. Stone (Christopher Lee) built look-alike robots to replace important people. In another, a villain created an automated house that was designed specifically to assassinate Mrs. Peel. A group of evil geniuses figured out how to make rain, and began drowning selected victims. And of course, the episodes with the Cybernauts are science fiction classics.

But even the vilest villains were invariably puns, too. A classic case: the foe was named Needles, and his hideout was a bunker buried under a pile of hay. So when Steed and Emma had to find Needles to stop him from blowing up the world or something, they had to look in ... a haystack.

TALKING HEADS

Among the most memorable children's shows of the '60s were a series of British science fiction adventures—"Supercar," "Fireball XL-5," "Stingray," and "Thunderbirds." Each featured a cast of eighteen-inch marionettes which, while not exactly lifelike, were impressively realistic. They blinked. They moved their eyes. They even seemed to be speaking their own dialogue.

The secret of this illusion, however, didn't rest only in the nimble hands of master puppeteers; technology had a hand, too. Gerry Anderson's marionettes were suspended by control wires (not thread) that actually triggered machinery hidden inside them. Through the wires, Anderson could transmit recorded speech to the mechanism that moved a marionette's mouth, thereby achieving a perfect synchronization between dialogue and lip movement. He called this technique "super-marionation."

Anderson didn't originally plan to spend his life working with marionettes. He wanted to break into the movie industry, but was offered the opportunity to do a children's puppet show instead. He accepted— although he knew nothing about puppets—and came up with a successful program called "Twizzle." This was followed by "Torchy the Battery Boy" and "Four Feather Falls," a marionette western.

"Supercar" was Anderson's fourth series and the turning point in his career. Frustrated by his inability to make mario-

Steve Zodiac, "Astronaut of the Year," hero of "Fireball XL-5," the only supermarionation series to be carried by a major American network. NBC aired it on Saturday mornings from 1963 to 1965. (Photo courtesy ITC Entertainment, Inc.)

nettes look like they were really walking, he decided to develop a program in which the characters spent most of their time sitting in a vehicle. So he created a fantasy car that could travel in the air or in water, as well as on land—Supercar.

The resulting series was staggeringly successful—a national phenomenon that became one of the most popular British kids' programs in history. Anderson realized that he'd stumbled on an ideal format—that science fiction was the perfect way to capitalize on a marionette's ability to "go" anywhere and "do" anything. So he continued experimenting with the genre, and over the next decade, developed many successful supermarionation sf series.

The continuing popularity of Anderson's creations is due primarily to two factors. First, the model work still ranks among the best ever done for TV. Each episode of an Anderson show required several new futuristic crafts—from high-tech road builders to starships—which had to be designed, built, and filmed in about a week. This took experts, and Anderson had them; his special effects people included Brian Johnson, who created the effects for *Aliens*, and Derek Meddings, who worked in the James Bond series and on *Superman I* and *II*. This duo pioneered the use of "lived in" models. Before them, TV props looked brand new and artificial. Anderson's team gave them a look that suggested realism: spaceships with discoloration from rocket blasts; cars with scratches and pits; even the characters had shadows under their eyes if they were supposed to be tired.

The second attraction of the programs is their unified, optimistic vision of the future. Almost every Anderson show takes place one hundred years from now. Each portrays mankind living in peace under the dominion of a benevolent world government. And in each, technology has become man's servant. For many sf fans, that kind of positive extrapolation is hard to resist—even when it's acted out only by marionettes.

The illusion of Supercar's flight was achieved by putting a model of the vehicle in front of a screen, then rear-projecting moving aerial footage onto it. Twenty thousand feet of sky footage were shot for the show. (Photo courtesy ITC Entertainment, Inc.)

SUPERCAR

TIME: The present.

PLACE: The American desert.

BACKGROUND: Somewhere in the American West is a laboratory owned and operated by two eccentric scientists, Dr. Beaker and Prof. Popkiss.

Working in seclusion, Beaker and Popkiss have invented the ultimate weapon—an indestructible automobile that can fly like a rocket and travel under water like a sub. They call it Supercar.

But it hasn't been tested yet, so they've hired daredevil Mike Mercury to take Supercar out on adventures, put it through its paces, and prove conclusively that the amazing vehicle can go anywhere and do anything.

HEROES:
•**Mike Mercury**: A bright and canny action hero—good-looking, intelligent, and absolutely fearless. Mercury can do almost anything: He's a great diver, a worldclass race-car driver, an ace pilot, and so on.
•**Jimmy**: A freckle-faced redhead around 11 years old whose brother was saved by Mercury. Accompanies Mike whenever the mission isn't too dangerous. Has a pet named **Mitch the Monkey**.

> *"What they had to work on was the story and characters; they already had the effects, because that's what puppets are all about."*
> —John Peel

VILLAINS:
•**Masterspy**: A big Sidney Greenstreet-type character who's after the secret of Supercar for himself. He has an incredibly inept sidekick called **Zarin**, a Peter Lorre character. They create crises, hoping Supercar will come to the rescue, then they try to steal it. Zarin's bumbling provides comic relief: Standard line: "Zarin, you fool. ... "

Mike Mercury climbs into Supercar for another test-drive in the sky. "Supercar" aired in Britain in 1961, and was syndicated in the U.S. the following year. There were thirty-nine episodes. (Photo courtesy ITC Entertainment, Inc.)

FIREBALL XL-5

"Fireball XL-5" was the first English show to have a robot as a continuing character. Here the faceless Robert acts as copilot with Steve Zodiac. There were thirty-nine episodes. (Photo courtesy ITC Entertainment, Inc.)

TIME: The 21st century.

PLACE: Outer space; and Space City, a community somewhere in the American desert (we see only about four or five buildings, but we're told that the astronauts live in houses dotted around the area).

BACKGROUND: In the twenty-first century, man is exploring space under the auspices of the WSP—the World Space Patrol—an international organization whose job is to protect Earth and expand human frontiers.

The W.S.P. headquarters, a revolving T-shaped building called the Control Tower, is located in Space City. It is the command center for a fleet of *X-L* spacecraft, sophisticated ships capable of faster-than-light travel. Our hero, Steve Zo-

diac is the pilot of *XL-5*. His mission: Patrol the galaxy, defend Earth, and answer distress calls.

IN SPACE: Like the U.S.S. *Enterprise, Fireball XL-5* doesn't land on planets. Instead, its nosecone detaches from the rest of the ship (this is called *Fireball, Jr.*), and is piloted onto planet surfaces. While on planets, the astronauts travel via jet-mobiles.

HEROES:
•**Col. Steve Zodiac**: Blond, bright, inventive, brave, chivalrous—100 percent hero, simply the greatest astronaut who's ever lived. Receives "Astronaut of the Year" award every year.

•**Venus**: Zodiac's copilot. Apparently French, but sounds Russian. A scientist and medical doctor, she's independent, competent, and good with a ray-gun. Her job is analyzing alien planets, life forms, etc. Naturally, she has a crush on Zodiac.
•**Prof. Matthew Matic**: Abbreviated, it's Math Matic. An eccentric genius, and designer of the *XL-5* (among other things). He's always working on Robert the Robot.
•**Robert the Robot** (voice supplied by Anderson): A transparent robot being trained to take over human work. Often rescues Steve and the Professor.

VILLAINS:
•**The Aliens of Planet 46**: Ugly, demonic humanoids who live in unbearably hot temperatures. They plan to destroy Earth.
•**Spacespy** and his wife, **Grizelda**: Inept freelance spies who are into stealing secrets, sabotage, etc. The usual stuff.

Several models of the *XL-5* were used. The smallest was six inches long. The largest was six feet long, and was operated by several people from the control gantry above it. The model was lifted by puppeteers as specially designed signal-rockets were fired by remote control, creating the illusion of flight. (Photo courtesy ITC Entertainment, Inc.)

STINGRAY

TIME: 21st century.

PLACE: Marineville, a city twenty miles inland on the Atlantic coast.

BACKGROUND: In the twenty-first century the surface world is at peace, united under a world government. Mankind has begun to explore the ocean and take mineral resources from it, but an undersea kingdom called Titanica is waging war on them.

To protect themselves, humans establish an ocean police force—the World Aquanaut Security Patrol (known as the WASPs). Their most powerful weapon: *Stingray*, a supersubmarine that can dive farther and move faster than any submarine ever built. Its sophisticated machinery includes an "automatic boatswain" autopilot, which enables the ship to be operated by two people. The pilot is Captain Troy Tempest.

STINGRAY'S MISSION: Police and patrol the sea, keep the seas safe for the nations of the world, and try to keep peace between the surface world and the undersea kingdoms.

HEROES:
•**Capt. Troy Tempest:** The "Aquanaut of the Year." Always has one eyebrow raised for some reason, making him look dashing. But he's a coward with women and has romantic problems; two girls are madly in love with him and he isn't sure which he prefers (a parody of American soap operas). Tempest has

a tendency to put his foot in his mouth. He's also a little irritable; he likes things to work out exactly right, and if they don't, he sulks.
•**"Phones" Sheriden:** Troy's assistant and copilot; works the hyrodophones (sonar equipment). Comes from the South and speaks with a drawl. A down-to-earth character, amiable, laid-back, and naive.
•**Marina:** A tailless, mute mermaid who used to be a Titanican slave. She's madly in love with Troy; she's also incredibly loyal to him, because he saved her life in the first episode.
•**Atlanta Shore:** Daughter of Commander **Sam Shore** (head

of the WASPs); also his assistant. She's all business, except where Troy is concerned—around him, she turns to jello. She and Marina are friendly rivals for Troy's attention.

VILLAINS:
•**Titan:** Green-skinned ruler of the undersea kingdom of Titanica, an evil despot out to rule the surface world—or destroy it. Only *Stingray* can stop him.
•**Agent X-20:** A bug-eyed blue amphibian who talks like Peter Lorre and spies on the surface people for Titan.
•**The Aquaphibians:** Titan's soldiers—big, green, and ugly, with bulging eyes, fangs, and fish rills down their backs. They ride inside "Terror Fish," big mechanical fish whose mouths open to fire missiles. They're stupid with a capital S.

"Stingray"'s thirty-nine episodes were shown in England in 1964, and syndicated in America in 1965. It was the first English program ever filmed in color. Although Anderson's troops had already faced and perfected many of the hardest supermarionation techniques, they ran into a new problem with this show: making the models look like they were under water. Their solution was to hold a piece of water-filled glass—sort of like a thin fish tank—in front of the camera. But even this wasn't an instant solution; a fish tank doesn't necessarily look like a miniature ocean. (Photo courtesy ITC Entertainment, Inc.)

THUNDERBIRDS

Left: The veddy sophisticated Lady Penelope was one of "Thunderbirds" most popular characters. The show was the first Anderson production to appeal to adults as well as children, and it's the most popular of all of his shows. "Thunderbirds" was originally planned as a half-hour adventure, but ITC president Lew Grade loved the rushes. "This is too damn good for half an hour," he said, and instructed Anderson to convert it into an hour-long show. That created a problem: Anderson's team had already completed a set of half-hour scripts, and couldn't afford to scrap them. So they went back and padded the first four episodes with dialogue. Instead of damaging the show, this accidentally saved it; the resulting character development is what made the program so popular. (Photo courtesy ITC Entertainment, Inc.)

TIME: 21st century.

PLACE: Earth and near space.

HEADQUARTERS: Tracy Island, a small island somewhere in the South Pacific.

BACKGROUND: Jeff Tracy, a millionaire ex-astronaut, has converted his private island into the headquarters of International Rescue—an organization composed exclusively of Tracy and his unusual family. There are four high-tech Thunderbird craft housed there; whenever a conventional rescue mission has failed, the Thunderbirds are called out.
•Thunderbird #1 is a vertical takeoff rocket plane capable of speeds in excess of 7,500 mph.
•Thunderbird #2 is a heavy carrier, hauling six interchangeable pods which contain machinery and material necessary

for any rescue mission—e.g., the "mole" for drilling.
•Thunderbird #3 is a spaceship, used primarily for near-space travel; it is launched from the island.
•Thunderbird #4 is a submarine, always transported by Thunderbird #2 to rescue sites.

There is a fifth Thunderbird craft, but #5 isn't on the island; it's a manned space station that monitors radio channels for distress signals. It is always in orbit.

HEROES:
•**Jeff Tracy**: A wealthy ex-astronaut and engineer. A firm, decisive, charsimatic individual; a man of action who sets his goal and achieves it.

The Thunderbirds are piloted by Tracy's five sons, all named

after former astronauts:
•**Scott Tracy**: The oldest and heir apparent, takes over Tracy Island in Jeff's absence. He's quick, alert, and decisive, just like dad.
•**Virgil Tracy**: The pilot of Thunderbird #2. Quiet, reserved; plays the piano. He's the only puppet on TV who ever smokes.
•**John Tracy**: Almost always on Thunderbird #5. A quiet loner who enjoys being by himself on the space station.
•**Gordon Tracy**: The pilot of Thunderbird #4, a nondescript character who doesn't turn up very often. He's a little impulsive and always feels he's being left out of missions. Travels in Thunderbird #2 as Virgil's assistant on rescue missions.
•**Alan Tracy**: The pilot of Thunderbird #3 and the baby of the family, a spoiled brat who gets away with whatever he wants. Petulant, headstrong,

six-wheeled Rolls Royce equipped with machine guns.

•**Parker**: Lady Penopelepe's butler, a reformed crook. He's an expert safecracker, a con artist, etc. He's also dedicated to Lady P. because she's the only person he's ever met who can best him.

VILLAINS:

The Hood: Master of disguise, a superspy with scores of plastic faces. Determined to steal the Thunderbirds' sophisticated secrets. He's also Kyrano's half brother and has some form of mental control over him. The Hood is the only surviving worshiper of a demonic god (nobody knows what it's called), so his headquarters are in an old temple in the jungles of Thailand.

Anderson spent between $60,000 and $70,000 for each of the thirty-two "Thunderbird" episodes. He used more than two hundred different models of the five Thunderbird vehicles, and had to hire one person just to make model chairs and upholster them. Above: the exterior of Thunderbird #1. Below: the interior, with Scott Tracy at the helm. (Photos courtesy ITC Entertainment, Inc.)

willful. He races cars for fun. He's the only brother with any romantic interest; he's in love with **Tin Tin** (Malaysian for "Sweet"), a beautiful, brilliant engineer who helps keep the Thunderbirds in working order. She's also the daughter of **Kryano**, Jeff's friend and butler.

OTHER CHARACTERS:

•**Brains**: An absolute genius who stammers because his mind works too fast for his mouth. He's blind without thick, horn-rimmed glasses. Very shy, withdrawn. Designed the Thunderbirds, and is constantly coming up with new inventions.

•**Lady Penelope Creighton-Ward**: A secret agent who works with International Rescue. She's very British, very upper crust; has a stately home, a butler ... the works. She's the Emma Peel ("The Avengers") type—beautiful, debonair, and lethal. Drives FAB-1, a shocking-pink

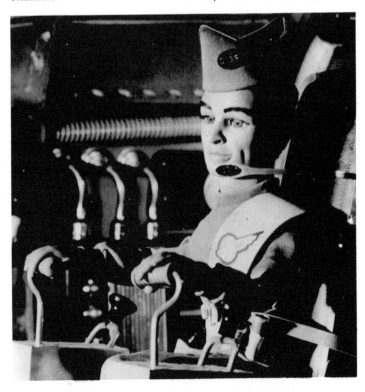

CAPTAIN SCARLET & THE MYSTERIONS

TIME: 21st century.

PLACE: Earth, the moon, and Mars (mostly Earth and Mars).

BACKGROUND: When Earth sent a peaceful expedition to Mars, the Mysterons—an advanced race of Martians with no physical form—mistakenly interpreted it as an unprovoked attack on their city. They vowed to destroy the human race in retaliation.

Now they're waging a war of nerves against the people of Earth, attacking little by little, taunting them with a warning before they strike (each episode begins with the warning).

The Mysterons wreak havoc by threatening to destroy the world's food supplies by killing all the plankton in the sea or threatening to assassinate an important leader. And in some episodes they actually succeed.

What makes the Mysterons dangerous is their power of "retro-metabolism." They can resurrect the dead, who then become the Mysterons' slaves in the war against Earth.

SPECTRUM: The only group that can prevent the Mysterons from destroying Earth is Spectrum, originally an international peacekeeping force, now the planet's last line of defense against alien invaders. Its headquarters is Cloudbase, a mobile platform suspended in the clouds using anitgravity. It can move anywhere on Earth.

AGENTS OF SPECTRUM (All Spectrum agents are named after colors):
•**Capt. Scarlet**: The top Spectrum agent; very intense, with no sense of humor. Scarlet is unique. He was actually killed and possessed by the Mysterons, but he was killed a second time in a battle and somehow—it's never explained how—he became both indestructible and free of their control. Now he can't be killed, so he takes every dangerous mission.
•**Capt. Blue**: An easy-going but incredibly effective agent. He's probably smarter than Scarlet and he's certainly more careful, because unlike Scarlet, he can be killed.

•**Colonel White**: The Commander of Spectrum; runs Cloudbase.
•**Captains Grey, Ochre, Magenta, Green**: Other agents.
•**Melody, Harmony, Symphony, Rhapsody, Destiny**: Five female pilots who fly Angel Interceptors and defend Cloudbase itself.

VILLAINS:
•**Mysterons**: Disembodied voices from Mars, determined to destroy the human race.
•**Capt. Black**: The Mysterons' human agent. He was formerly Spectrum's top agent, and he's not intentionally a traitor; he was killed and possessed by the Martians. Looks like a zombie, and speaks with a deep, gravelly voice that suggests he's dead. He's sort of a vampire, because he kills people and brings them back to life as Mysteron agents. Black turns up wherever there's death.

Anderson's marionettes got more sophisticated with each show. By the time he got to "Captain Scarlet," they were perfectly proportioned. And each one was designed to look like the actor whose voice was being used. "Normally," says Ed (Captain Blue) Bishop, "other puppet programs would do the puppets first and then have the actors match their voices to the puppets. Gerry's people made the puppets work to the persona of the actors. ... We were all amazed by it." "Captain Scarlet"'s twenty-six episodes were syndicated in America in 1967. (Photo courtesy ITC Entertainment, Inc.)

SHORT TAKES

Short stories are a staple of science fiction literature, but their TV counterparts, sf anthology programs, haven't met with as much success. Out of the dozen or so that have been produced in the last thirty-five years, few have lasted more than a season and hardly any have resurfaced in reruns. As a result, most contemporary sf fans will never see many of the best.

Nonetheless, about 25 percent of the participants in this poll included little-known anthology programs in their lists of top sf shows. And some, like author Bill Warren (*Keep Watching the Skies!*), even expressed a preference for them.

"Obviously," Warren says, "there are built-in limitations to a continuing character series:

"First, you can never put any of the leading characters in genuine peril.

"Second, you're limited to dealing with the time and setting of the characters.

"And third, you're limited to the same characters every week.

"But an anthology show can range from the beginning to the end of time. It can have new and different characters every week. And the stories don't have to be upbeat, like most regular series have to be. In terms of science fiction, this flexiblity makes anthology shows vastly preferable to character shows. But obviously the viewing public doesn't care for them."

Michael Duffy, of the *Detroit Free Press*, adds: "Flexibility makes anthologies interesting, but it's also probably the reason they haven't worked in the ratings. The mass audience has become so attuned to seeing the same characters doing the same things week after week that they're not capable of sticking with a show that gives them different characters, different stories, and different situations—especially ones that are likely to come at them in an unexpected fashion."

So, many of the critics' favorite anthologies, like "Way Out" and "Science Fiction Theater," remain cult secrets.

"The best anthology series on television is unquestionably HBO's "Ray Bradbury Theatre," wrote *Cinefantastique* magazine in 1986. Above, three scenes from the series. Clockwise, from left: Bestial children from the episode "The Playground"; Peter O'Toole in "Banshee"; and Drew Barrymore in "The Screaming Woman." (Photos courtesy Atlantis Films, Ltd.)

NIGHT GALLERY

Critics—including Rod Serling, left—panned "Night Gallery." "I did a show called 'The Different Ones,' he told a reporter in his last interview ever, "about a boy who was a freak and was ultimately sent to a different planet where he would be more accepted. It was beautiful, a very sensitive screenplay which was a piece of s_ _t when it was done. It was a ... bug-eyed monster kind of film, which it wasn't supposed to be at all." Nonetheless, the show lasted for three years and ninety episodes. The first two seasons were an hour long, the last was a half hour. Below: a "Night Gallery" PR shot.

"Rod Serling's Night Gallery" was the master's return to anthology TV. Actually, it was more like Boris Karloff's "Thriller" than "Twilight Zone." The stories were only occasionally science fiction (its emphasis was on the supernatural), and Serling had increasingly little to do with it—he sold it to NBC, which proceeded to reject most of his scripts and even prevented him from attending casting sessions. Serling retaliated by trying to remove his name from the series, but he was under contract to appear as its host, and had no choice but to fulfill his obligations to the network.

The series originally aired in 1970 as part of an NBC experiment called "Four In One"—four hour-long series (including "McCloud"), each of which aired once a month. It became a regular series in the 1971–72 season, and the following year it became a half-hour show. Serling was disgusted by the whole experience; he left television for good when "Night Gallery" was cancelled. It wasn't a total loss, though; Serling named a "Night Gallery" episode called "They're Tearing Down Tim Riley's Bar" as a personal favorite among all the shows he wrote.

A CRITIC'S COMMENT

" 'Twilight Zone' was usually ironic. 'Night Gallery' was often just depressing, with very dark stories and very downbeat endings—cases where nobody won. It was like the dark side of Rod Serling. And you know, by then his career wasn't flourishing—he'd run into some problems and I think it showed up in his work. He didn't really have a lot to do with writing many of the shows, but I think he set the tone. I liked it because I thought it was a real change for television to have something so dark.

"There were some really fine actors and actresses in it, many of whom were just getting started. And it had very offbeat stories—things you don't normally see on TV, where it's twenty-two minutes to get to a happy ending. These were the other side of humanity. A nice change."
—**Bob Wisehart,** *Sacramento Bee*

WAY OUT

At 9:30 on Friday nights in 1961, just before "Twilight Zone" came on, you could *really* scare yourself by tuning in this collection of bizarre stories written and introduced by black humorist/novelist Roald Dahl. CBS was obviously trying to duplicate "Twilight Zone" 's appeal; like Serling's half hour, Dahl's was resolutely intelligent. But "Way Out" wasn't offering any gentle morality plays, as "Twilight Zone" often did. Dahl (whose short stories included "Lamb to the Slaughter," which was adapted into the most famous "Alfred Hitchcock Presents" episode) wrote about peculiar subjects in a grim and morbid fashion. The stories weren't about sad things happening to sad people—they were about *terrible* things happening to *terrible* people. Naturally, it didn't go over too well with the masses. After a little more than three months on the air, "Way Out" was dead and buried.

> "TV science fiction, generally, is pinned to a singular gimmick that wears thin after more than two or three episodes. In the anthology format, you can change gimmicks every week, like underwear."
>
> —Michael Dougan, *S.F. Examiner*

A CRITIC'S COMMENT

" 'Way Out' was very quiet and low-key. But it was really scary.

"I remember tuning into the first one, which turned out to be a remake of 'Donovan's Brain.' I was so terrified by the idea that they were going to remove this guy's brain and put it in a tank that I couldn't watch.

"A little while later, they had an episode in which the main character was experimenting with a machine that would tame wild animals. He had a real nasty wife who would keep coming into the laboratory at lunch hour and bitching at him, so he put her in the machine. It worked; she became very tame, very docile, very placid. But unfortunately, the side-effect was that she couldn't stand anything that *wasn't* tame, docile and placid. If you got rowdy on her, she would kill you—which is eventually what happened.

"The final episode I will always remember. It took place in a photographer's studio. The photographer's wife and his partner were planning to run away together. Meanwhile, the photographer had discovered this retouching fluid which, when you applied it to a picture, worked on the subject of the photo as well as the photo itself. So he made himself look younger, and made his wife look older and ruined her relationship with his partner, who didn't want her after she'd lost her looks. Infuriated, she went back into the studio and confronted the photographer—and poured the retouching fluid all over *his* picture. It blanked out half his face. I remember the moment when he turned toward the camera. He only had one eye and the corner of a mouth left. I don't recall if the makeup was any good or not—but it didn't matter; I was haunted by that shot for years afterward.

"As far as I know, 'Way Out' has never been shown in syndication, and I've never seen any episodes at science fiction conventions. So I don't know how it would hold up today. I think there probably wasn't a lot of money being spent on *things*— on sets or costumes. And I don't recall any really famous people appearing in it; I can't even say with any certainty how good the acting was.

"But the fact that the stories have stuck with me as long as they have is, I think, indicative of how well written they were. There was so much more attention paid to setting up a situation and getting you to believe it while you were watching it than there is in most shows. The result … well, they still haunt me."

—**Pat Cadigan, SF Writer**

ONE STEP BEYOND

Jack Lord made one of his first TV appearances on "One Step Beyond." Other future stars who can be seen in the show include Warren Beatty, Louise Fletcher, Christopher Lee, and Elizabeth Montgomery.

"Have you ever been certain the telephone would ring within the next ten seconds? Or have you ever walked down a street and had the feeling you knew what lay beyond the unturned corner? Then you've had a brief encounter with the unknown, a small step beyond. Now take a giant one."

With that, host John Newland would usher his audience into another chilling half hour of "Alcoa Presents"—better known as "One Step Beyond."

Newland's sardonic sense of humor permeated the show; you could tell that the guy liked giving you the creeps. Even in the show's TV ads, he was spooky. One showed him sitting on the ledge of an apartment building, about twenty floors up. "Haven't you ever had the urge to jump?" he asked. And after his pitch for the show, that's exactly what

he did.

"One Step Beyond" can only be marginally termed science fiction, although it was listed frequently in this sf poll. Its bailiwick was the supernatural, psychic phenomena, ESP, reincarnation. And rather than fiction, it purported to be based on fact. Episodes might explore the supernatural experiences connected with Abraham Lincoln's death, or tell the true story of a child seen hitchhiking a year after she died. And there were a healthy number of "Telltale Heart" stories, with guilty murderers being haunted by apparitions of their victims. There was even a Bigfoot episode. But this wasn't *National Enquirer* television. "One Step Beyond" was a genuinely scary look into the world below your mind.

In "The Dark Room," dark-haired Cloris Leachman portrayed a photographer who was terrified of a strangler.

The sardonic Mr. Newland, host and director of "One Step Beyond." In the '80s, while "Twilight Zone" and "Alfred Hitchcock Presents" were being revived, Newland came back with a new version of this show, too. Unfortunately, it didn't remain in production.

But were they really true? Newland provided corroborative material, and science fiction writer Peter Pautz actually checked out some of his references.

"I followed up on a few of them," he says, "and found cases that were documented. There was one episode in particular where the narrator talked about a book predicting the sinking of the *Titanic*, describing its length, the number of stacks, how many people died, and all that. He said it was written by a guy named Richard Johnson, that the ship in the book was called the *Titan*—and it was written twelve years before the *Titanic* sank. So I went back and researched it and found that the book did indeed exist—it took about two months to find a copy. And it was published in 1901, just as Newland said!" Eerie music, please.

SCIENCE FICTION THEATRE

Left: In a 1961 episode of "One Step Beyond," "The Last Round," a young Charles Bronson lived up to his tough guy image by playing a boxer. 1960-61 was the show's last season; after two and a half years and ninety-one episodes, it was cancelled.

What could "Flipper" and "Science Fiction Theater" have in common? They were both produced by Ivan Tors.

In 1955, Tors created this low-budget excercise in scientific extrapolation. Each story was based on fact; technical advisers included leading scientists; and it was presented as a quasi-documentary.

Many of the show's stories, in fact, introduced inventions that have since become reality. "One episode," says critic Allen Asherman, "featured an aging policeman ... who learns he has a heart condition. To permit his doctor to keep track of his condition while he's working, the policeman is outfitted with an electronic belt. The doctor, at a receiving station in his office, can monitor the heartbeat. Today, this machinery ... is used to monitor the heartbeats of intensive-care patients."

The host and narrator of "SF Theater" was newsman Truman Bradley. It was produced from 1955 to 1957, and aired exclusively as a syndicated program. Half the seventy-eight episodes were in color.

A CRITIC'S COMMENTS:

" 'Science Fiction Theater' treated science fiction concepts realistically and honestly, sometimes even timidly. ... It was a low budget show with no special effects to speak of, and no location work ... .

"It first appeared in 1955, and at that time, all science fiction on television—'Captain Video,' 'Space Patrol,' and the rest— was aimed directly at children. This was the only sf show on the air, between a couple of the very early ones and 'Twilight Zone,' that was for adults.

"The two best episodes were similar in content. The first one was called 'Time Is Just Its Life." It's about a couple—the husband/hero is actually a science fiction writer—who notice that the people next door are a little strange. The hero eventually realizes that his neighbors are fleeing from an oppressive future, and as he watches, at the end, they're caught by the Time Police and taken back. A strange, haunting concept, but it was all very low-key—which the producers thought was necessary in order to appeal to grown-ups of that period.

"The other episode is called "Strange People at Pecos,' in which a family appears to be aliens. This causes the children in town to turn against the little girl of the family, and the adults become very suspicious of the little girl's parents. At the end, it turns out that they're probably not from outer space—but only probably. The producers left the door open to speculation.

"Generally, 'Science Fiction Theater' was very positive about science; scientists were almost invariably the heroes. Its major message was that science is good; that scientists are helping people, that advances in science are advancements for the average person. And it said that we have nothing to fear from the future."

—**Bill Warren,**
Keep Watching the Skies!

C A R T O O N S

There have been dozens of science fiction cartoon series on TV. Four prominent sf magazine editors nominated the following shows as the best and the worst of the lot.

"Jonny Quest": © 1987 Hanna-Barbera Productions, Inc.

THE BEST

JONNY QUEST
Premiere: 1964
Hanna-Barbera's prime-time animated tale of a 12-year-old who traveled around the world with his scientist/detective father, Dr. Benton Quest. Their extended family included Roger "Race" Bannon, their bodyguard/muscleman; Hadji, an adopted Indian boy; and their dog, Bandit. It was inspired by Milton Caniff's "Terry and the Pirates," and judging from poll results, it is one of the most highly respected sf cartoons ever made.

A CRITIC'S COMMENTS:
" 'Jonny Quest' was really the first attempt at an intelligent science fiction prime-time cartoon. ... It came at a time when very few shows presented scientists in a favorable light. They were always either evil or they were bumbling old professor - types who simply offered advice here and there. But Dr. Quest, a middle-aged scientist, was an intelligent and thoughtful character—a role model for pre-teens. I identified with him, and I think that might have been a major factor in *my* decision to become a scientist. Today I'm the director of scientific affairs for a major trade association."
—D. Douglas Fratz, *Thrust* magazine

STAR TREK
Premiere: 1973
Most of the original "Star Trek" cast supplied voices for this Filmation adaptation of the series. It helped introduce the original show to a new generation of American kids and won an Emmy in 1975.

THUNDARR THE BARBARIAN
Premiere: 1980
A Conan-style character of the future. In 1994, a comet wiped out all civilization on Earth. Two thousand years later, its population includes mutants, monsters, and wizards. Thundarr roams the world taking on the forces of evil and defending other slaves.

SPACE GHOST
Premiere: 1966
Hanna-Barbera's popular interplanetary hero possesses a magic belt that makes him invisible. He travels with two teenage assistants, Jan and Jayce, and a pet space monkey named Blip. Space Ghost's voice was supplied by "Laugh-In"'s Gary Owens. The character is currently enjoying a comic book revival.

"Space Ghost": © 1987 Hanna-Barbera Productions, Inc.

CARTOONS

STAR BLAZERS
Premiere: 1979
A syndicated series that originally achieved tremendous poularity in Japan under the name "Space Cruiser Yamato."

FLASH GORDON
Premiere: 1979
Animated version of the classic sf comic strip and movie serial, produced by Filmation. Flash, an astronaut, defends Earth from space villains like Ming the Merciless.

ROCKY AND BULLWINKLE
Premiere: 1959
It's not pure sf, but Sherman and Mr. Peabody regularly journeyed into the past in the WABAC machine; Rocky and Bullwinkle pursued the Mooseberry bush, which was used to make rocket fuel; and Gidney and Cloyd visited from the moon. It's a great series.

THE WORST

SPACE KIDDETTES
Premiere: 1966
A series about a bunch of teenage outer-space crime fighters named Snoopy, Countdown, Pupstar, Scooter, Jenny, and Captain Skyhook.

DODO, THE KID FROM OUTER SPACE
Premiere: 1967
Dodo, a native of the planet Hena Hydo, arrives on Earth with his pet, Compy, to give old Professor Fingers a hand with scientific experiments.

GILLIGAN'S PLANET
Premiere: 1982
Gilligan shows up in outer space, stranded on a far-off planet. No matter how lost he gets, he always winds up on TV somehow.

JOSIE AND THE PUSSYCATS IN OUTER SPACE
Premiere: 1972
A spinoff of the "Archie" series. An all-girl rock group posing for publicity shots on a NASA rocket accidentally gets shot into space.

GODZILLA POWER HOUR
Premiere: 1979
Godzilla is a friendly creature from the deep who assists his pals—a bunch of oceanographers resembling Jacques Cousteau's crew.

YOGI'S SPACE RACE
Premiere: 1978
Yogi and Boo-Boo are great characters, but they belong in Jellystone Park. What are they doing in space?

LOOKING BACK

It's hard to say when the Space Age really began. America fired its first Redstone rocket in 1952; Russia sent the first man-made satellite into orbit in 1957. But Tom Corbett and Buzz Corry took off for the far reaches of the universe in 1950, and millions of young dreamers went with them.

There were about a dozen live space operas on the air between 1950 and 1955. Although these shows were generally optimistic about the future (in virtually all of them, the nations of Earth had joined together to establish a world government), not everyone found them attractive. "A change has taken place in the nature of the visual entertainment offered our young people," wrote an alarmed reviewer in 1951. "Now we have a vogue for drama dealing with interpanetary travel centuries hence—shattering episodes involving screeching rockets, crackling ray-guns, and plastic-helmeted adventurers."

He could never have guessed how far-reaching the effects of these shows would actually be.

Twenty-five years later, author John Davis summed it up in *The TV Book*: "It can reasonably be asked," he wrote "if there would be any space program or any NASA today without the television space shows of the fifties. … For members of the postwar baby boom, the first generation to grow up with television, it was the Saturday morning space operas that captured our imaginations and got us excited about the concept of man traveling through the inky reaches of out-

Steve Holland played Flash Gordon in a syndicated series in 1953.

er space." Television helped make it convincing. "It [seemed] fitting," Davis explains, "that the wonders of tomorrow should be shown to us on the greatest scientific wonder of the day—as was attested to by the appropriate title of the first of the television space shows, 'Captain Video.'"

Space operas in television's Golden Age may have inspired future scientists, but they were hardly educational. Most were wild fantasies that ignored even the most elementary natural laws. "Even an eleven-year-old could catch scores of ridiculous inaccuracies," Davis recalls; "things like smoke rising from a rocket's exhaust, ray-guns making nice sizzling sounds in what was supposed to be the vacuum of space, or a giant hole being blown in the side of a spaceship without everything inside being instantly sucked out." But that didn't really matter. In 1950, it was the vision of space travel—

not the details—that counted.

Besides "Captain Video," there were two significant space operas: "Tom Corbett, Space Cadet," and "Space Patrol." "Corbett" had the superior special effects, using a two-camera technique that superimposed actors' images onto an entirely separate set. So even in live TV, it was possible for producers to make Tom and his crew "float weightlessly" in space, or walk in a "tunnel under the moon." "Corbett" also aimed for unprecedented scientific accuracy by hiring renowned rocket expert Willy Ley as a consultant.

But "Space Patrol" was the real forerunner to modern sf programs. Its themes—"a planet whose inhabitants had been reduced to savagery by nuclear war," or "a thinking crystal that believed it was God"—were remarkably sophisticated. "I could take the characters from 'Space Patrol' and put them on the *Enterprise* today without any problem," says "Star Trek" writer David Gerrold, a boyhood fan. And indirectly, he probably already has.

On board the Orbit Jet with Rocky Jones in 1954.

JOHNNY JUPITER

TIME: 1953

PLACE: Anywhere, USA.

BACKGROUND: "Johnny Jupiter" was TV's first science fiction puppet show. It had two incarnations: From March to June 1953, it was broadcast live on the DuMont network; from September 1953 to May 1954, it was shown in a filmed version. The format was slightly different for each series. In the first, Ernest P. Duckweather, janitor in a TV studio, was messing with the dials in the control room one night pretending to be a producer. He accidentally tuned in the planet Jupiter and got three Jovians (puppets in real life) on the screen: Johnny Jupiter, B-12, and B-12's robot, Major Domo. They became TV pals, and thereafter spent their evenings in interplanetary conversation.

With the live show's success, "Johnny Jupiter" 's creators had visions of owning a new "Howdy Doody." So they filmed it for syndication, removing much of the satire and replacing it with slapstick. In the new version, the hero was a clerk in the Frisbee General Store who liked to tinker with machines and invent weird gadgets. One of his gadgets turned out to be a television which enabled him to speak with Jupiter, etc. Unfortunately, it lasted only another year.

THE CHARACTERS:
• **Ernest P. Duckweather** (Wright King): A lovable nerd who wants to do the right thing, but doesn't have the savoir faire to pull it off. He's not too good with girls, but he's terrific with machines.
• **Johnny Jupiter** (a hand puppet): A creature from Jupiter with a bulbous head and a narrow face. His suggestions often help Duckweather solve personal problems (like how to get along with his girlfriend), but he's got a quirky sense of humor that's just as likely to get Duckweather into trouble.
• **B-12** (a puppet): Johnny's sardonic butler-type sidekick.
• **Major Domo** (a puppet): B-12's robot, the resident dumbo.

A CRITIC'S COMMENT

In his book, Saturday Morning TV, *"Entertainment This Week" producer Gary H. Grossman recalled TV's first science fiction puppet show. An excerpt follows.*

" 'Johnny Jupiter,' [*New York Times* TV critic Jack] Gould wrote in 1953, was a 'delightfully wild item of video fantasy that has charm, intelligence, and a wonderful satirical point of view. It is something not to be missed.'

Johnny's and B-12's attacks on Earth were strictly verbal. They criticized taxation and television. The planet Jupiter, they said, had television, but it is used for punishing children when they spend too much time reading books or playing with slide rules.

Johnny explained that he couldn't understand why Earth has any traffic problems. Vehicular congestion on Jupiter was solved simply by picking the most crowded street and erecting signs that read, 'Parking Allowed.' And the Jupiterian wondered why Earthlings made such a fuss for a beautiful woman, when it is the homely girl who needs attention.

One week Duckweather auditioned for a TV news program on Jupiter and ended up satirizing American commentators and the pressure brought to bear by special interest groups. As Duckweather announced an item about a pair of moon dwellers apprehended by the satellite patrol, the Moon Dwellers Association telephoned to protest. The item was dropped. Next he began 'a shocking expose about underwater plant life' that was greeted by objections from the Underwater Vegetable League. He killed the story. 'And here's a juicy tidbit,' continued Duckweather, only to be stopped in midsentence by the Juicy Tidbit Society. Duckweather signed off with a song entitled, 'The Program That Doesn't Offend.' "

SPACE PATROL

Commander Corry and crew piloted the Terra through six years of radio and television; "Space Patrol" debuted on ABC in 1950, and finally disappeared in 1956. In its prime, the show was successful enough to justify a huge $25,000-per-week budget.

A CRITIC'S COMMENT

" 'Space Patrol' was the first attempt to do serious science fiction on television with continuing characters. 'Star Trek' owes a lot to it. 'Space Patrol' was a fifteen-minute-a-night serial, five times a week, and they did it live; there was no tape. They had bare walls for sets and occasionally a desk ... they had a model of a space ship with a cutout window and a couple of levers, a repellor ray, and whatever else. It was all very simplistic. ... But over a period of time, they did stories about suspended animation, about cloning, about an incredible energy matrix which was eating the universe. There was one which was very much like *The Invasion of the Body Snatchers*—if you fell asleep, someone could take over your body; they did a story like *The Crucible*, where they went back in time to sixteenth century Salem during the time of the witch hunts, and a woman who tried to tell someone about this spaceship she'd seen was going to be tried as a witch. And this was during the height of the McCarthy era. So 'Space Patrol' was doing the same thing that 'Star Trek' later did—it was commenting on what was going on in the world through science fiction terms. It was way ahead of its time. It's a brilliant show, deserving of far more credit than it has ever been given, because it had such impact on its viewing audience."

—**David Gerrold,**
Screenwriter/SF *Writer*

TIME: The 30th century.

PLACE: Our solar system.

BACKGROUND: In the thirtieth century, five worlds—Earth, Mars, Jupiter, Mercury, and Venus—banded together to form the United Planets of the Universe, an Earth-based political organization resembling the ancient United Nations.

Inhabitants of the United Planets coexisted in peace, but to protect themselves—and the rest of the solar system—from an assortment of space desperadoes, the UP established an interplanetary military force called the Space Patrol.

THE SPACE PATROL: Based on an artifical planetoid located between the orbits of Earth and Mars, *Terra Station* (its core was built out of the soils of all of Earth's nations, symbolizing the show's "one world" concept), the Space Patrol keeps law and order in the universe, answers distress calls, and runs sensitive errands for the Secretary General of the U.P. The pride of their rocket fleet is the *Terra V*, piloted by the show's two main characters:

•**Commander in Chief Buzz Corry** (Ed Kemmer): The Captain Kirk of his era, an intrepid, compassionate leader with a square jaw, clean mind, hard punch, and infallible judgment. He knows how to get the job done, and gets it done right. Unquestionably the best pilot in the galaxy.

•**Cadet Happy** (Lyn Osborn): Buzz's devoted young copilot, a space teenager with his own hip language, like "Smokin' rockets!" (Earth translation: "Holy cow!"), and "Blast off!"

(translation: "Beat it!"). He worships Buzz. He also asks a lot of simple questions so the Commander can explain things to the kids in the audience.

SUPPORTING CAST:
• **Carol Karlyle** (Virginia Hewitt): The beautiful daughter of the Secretary General of the UP Of course, she's in love with Buzz.
• **Major Robbie Robertson** (Ken Mayer): Security Chief of the Universe.
• **Mr. Karlyle** (Norman Jolley): Secretary General of the U.P.
• **Tonga** (Nina Bara): Formerly an arch-villainess who underwent Brainograph treatment to remove her antisocial tendencies (in the thirtieth century, criminals are rehabilitated mechanically). Now she's become a Space Patrol ally.

THE VILLAINS:
"Space Patrol" featured some of the cosmos' nastiest criminals:

•**Prince Baccarratti** (Bela Kovacs): Corry's arch-enemy, a lean, effusive megalomaniac known as The Black Falcon; the "diabolical pretender to the Venusian throne." He is evil incarnate, the prototype Klingon. Ousted from his asteroid stronghold by the Space Patrol early in the series, he has sworn revenge on Corry.

Prince Baccaratti was played by the show's associate producer. To appear properly evil, he combed his hair forward so there was a tangled mop of it resting on his forehead. He also played the prince with an accent; he had to, since he was from Czechoslovakia and normally spoke with a heavy accent anyway.

•**Malengro** (Larry Dobkins): Baccarrati's evil genius sidekick.

•**Mr. Proteus** (Marvin Miller): A master of disguises, He was played by the actor who became the star of "The Millionaire" in 1955.

Above: "Space Patrol" spawned "Rocky Jones," the spaceman in a baseball cap. Played by Richard Crane, Rocky blasted off in 1954, just as the space fad was running out of fuel. It lasted thirty-one episodes.

Below: Buzz and Carol read over a scene on the set of "Space Patrol." Originally, every script was written by Mike Moser, the Navy Air Force pilot who created the show. Eventually, radio and TV commitments totaled more than 82,000 words every week, and Moser had to hire three writers.

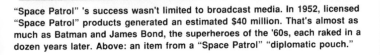

"Space Patrol" 's success wasn't limited to broadcast media. In 1952, licensed "Space Patrol" products generated an estimated $40 million. That's almost as much as Batman and James Bond, the superheroes of the '60s, each raked in a dozen years later. Above: an item from a "Space Patrol" "diplomatic pouch."

TOM CORBETT, SPACE CADET

"Tom Corbett, Space Cadet" has the distinction of being the only program ever to air on all four networks. It premiered on CBS in 1950 as a three-times-a-week adventure, Monday, Wednesday and Friday at 6:45 P.M. Then it moved to ABC at the same time, until 1952. (Meanwhile, NBC had picked up an edited kinescope of the weekday telecasts for Saturday mornings.) In 1953, DuMont aired it; but in 1954 NBC took it away from the ailing fourth network and broadcast it until June, 1955—when Tom and his crew blasted off for the last time.

TIME: 400 years in the future (2350 to 2355 AD).

PLACE: Based on Earth, but most of the action takes place in space.

BACKGROUND: "Tom Corbett" was loosely adapted from Robert Heinlein's 1948 novel, *Space Cadet*.

In the twenty-fourth century, Earth is at peace. All nations have joined together to form the Commonwealth of Earth, and they have colonized "Mars, Venus, and Titan, a satellite of Saturn"—which now make up the Solar Alliance.

On Earth, Tom Corbett and his fellow cadets attend Space Academy USA, the West Point of the future and "the best school in the universe." When they graduate, they'll join the Solar Guards, "peace-enforcement unit of the Solar Alliance," whose job is to "maintain peace on the colonized planets and explore the possiblity of colonizing others." In the meantime, Tom and the crew of his ship, the *Polaris*, go on training missions that are as good as real adventures.

HEROES:

•**Tom Corbett** (Frankie Thomas): A teenage Space Cadet (Thomas was really in his early twenties) and a crack pilot. He's a regular guy who's mature beyond his years—so other cadets look up to him and his instructors at the academy give him plenty of responsibility. A real leader.

•**Cadet Roger Manning** (Jan Merlin): The wise-guy gunner of

A CRITIC'S COMMENT

"While the hero on 'Space Patrol' was a commander, Tom Corbett was a cadet. He was sort of a junior astronaut (although the term *astronaut* wasn't actually coined until 1959), which made him more like us, the audience, who had refrigerator boxes in our basements painted or cut out to look like rocket ships, and who pretended that we were spacemen. Tom was a teenager, yet he was able to have his own adventures. He got in and out of trouble on his own (or with the other cadets) and he made his own decisions. Occasionally there were adult characters around, but more often than not it was the cadets themselves who were piloting spaceships. And the other cadets represented all the types of kids we played with: There were good kids, bullies, kids who couldn't quite make a decision about things, kids who needed to be given a chance. Most episodes on Tom Corbett tended to deal with kid concerns, so it was a program we could really relate to."

—**Helene Seifer,**
TV Producer

Tom's crew. Quick-tempered, impetuous, brave, but a pain in the butt; sort of the Eddie Haskell of the twenty-fourth century.
•**Cadet Astro** (Al Markim): A Venusian. The exact opposite of Manning—he's pleasant, quiet, reasonable. Tom's navigator.

SUPPORTING CAST:
•**Commander Arkwright** (Carter Blake): The man in charge of Space Academy,USA.
•**Capt. Steve Strong** (Michael Harvey/Edward Bryce).
•**Dr. Joan Dale** (Margaret Garland): A teacher at Space Academy and Tom's girlfriend.
•**Cadet Rattison** (Frank Sutton): Graduated to the US Marines to become Gomer Pyle's drill sergeant.

THE VILLAINS:
Unlike in "Space Patrol," there are more environmental and technical problems to overcome on "Tom Corbett" than there are villains. In fact, there are no regular villains at all. There *is* an asteroid belt between Mars and Jupiter that serves as a hideout for various space crooks; Tom takes them on every once in a while. And in one episode, Tom fought the stickmen, which were "literally stick men moving over a black background." Other foes fall into the "prehistoric monster in space" genre.

The Official "Tom Corbett Space Cadet" ring.

Above: Tom Corbett calls Earth. Some space operas disregarded scientific facts completely, but "Tom Corbett" actually hired rocket expert Willy Ley to consult on its scripts, helping to keep the stories within the realm of possibility (if not probability). "The writers are always wanting their ship to hit something out in space," he said in 1951. "Thank God I've got them to stop hitting asteroids for a while. The probabilities of a spaceship's encountering an asteroid in its path, you know, are so slight as to be negligible. The writers were overdoing it. They wanted to hit an asteroid practically every week. 'Please, boys,' I told them. 'Only once or twice a year.' "

Right: When Tom readied the Polaris for takeoff, he was rarely headed into battle. So in "Tom Corbett," like "Space Patrol," people rarely died. Explained the script editor in 1951: "No gore in this show. ... We lay off horror. So far, we've had only one death on the show, and that was accidental." It happened on the planet Mercury during a war. "It wasn't even a war. More like a skirmish, come to think of it," the script editor mused. "The Mercurians had misinterpreted a visit by the Space Cadets, and thought it was an invasion. In the scuffle that followed, one of the Mercurians collapsed."

CULT FAVORITES

TOM CORBETT: ON THE SET

Thomas Whiteside, of The New Yorker *magazine, visited the set of "Tom Corbett" in 1951. A few of his notes:*

"[Producer Allen] Ducovny took me on a tour of the studio to examine some of the props. These included a dirty tennis ball which, suspended from an easel by a thread, would represent a planet; an old Edison Voice writer with a roll of paper in it which would represent an electronic machine at Space Academy that automatically typed out oral reports relayed to it from space by radio; and a pile of switches and magnetic coils, handily mounted, Ducovny explained, for ready attachment to anything around the studio that might need an extra electronic touch. Stopping behind a small model of a rocket ship, Ducovny showed me a DDT bomb concealed behind it. 'We used this model for shooting takeoffs and landings,' he said. 'You get a swell white blast from the DDT bomb that looks like the real thing. Once we tried out a perfume bomb for a takeoff scene, because it had a nice dense spray, but the actors yelled blue murder and we had to go back to DDT. And *that* doesn't smell too good, either.'"

"[Frankie] Thomas, like the others, was dressed in light-gray Space Cadet fatigues. He also wore a wide leather belt to which were attached an oven thermometer, a five-inch long metal tube, an underwater swimming mask, a soldering iron with a transparent Lucite muzzle and with spiral springs decorating its barrel, and a miniature hammer, like the ones used to break the glass of fire-alarm boxes. Aside from the hammer, the significance of which, I discovered, nobody connected with the show could explain, these accoutrements represented, respectively, a Geiger counter, an electroscopic magnifier, an oxygen mask, and a Paralo-Ray gun."

In one episode, Tom and his crew "landed" on a planet of dinosaurs.

"The actors walked off and began their rehearsal. The Mesozoic explorations of Tom Corbett and his crew evidently were beginning to bear fruit. The actors crouched around the big footprint painted on the floor.

'Great rings of Saturn!' one of them exclaimed. 'What do you make of it, Tom?'

'Looks like a footprint to me,' Tom Corbett said.

With that, a roar of wild beasts burst from a loudspeaker overhead.

'Great Jupiter!' another Space Cadet cried, jerking his soldering iron from its holster and aiming it. As he aimed, a series of ominous crackling and buzzing sounds rose above the din from the loudspeaker, and then the roars died away.

'Great Galaxy! A dinosaur!' Tom Corbett said, peering into the jungle. 'Thank Jupiter those Paralo-Rays took effect!' "

Good thing the paralo-rays took effect, all right. Otherwise millions of kids would have realized that Tom was fighting a little plastic dinosaur that couldn't have moved if he'd begged it to.

Tom and his "girlfriend," Dr. Joan Dale.

ODDS & ENDS

The Rocket Rangers at the control panel of their spaceship, the Beta. Left to right: actors Cliff Robertson, Jack Weston, John Boruff, and Bruce Hall.

It's only TV: "I don't know a logarithm from a rocket sled," television astronaut William Lundigan told TV Guide in 1959. "It's all I can do to drive a car."

"ROD BROWN OF THE ROCKET RANGERS" is one of the best-known of the early science fiction TV programs—not because it was particularly good, but because it was the only one to claim a future Oscar-winner among its regular cast: Cliff Robertson, who won for his role in *Charley,* played the lead character. During the year in which he explored the galaxy every Saturday morning, Robertson was simultaneously costarring in a Broadway play with Elizabeth Montgomery and studying at the Actor's Workshop. "Sharpening three edges of the sword," he called it.

"Commando Cody, Sky Marshal of the Universe" (right) aired briefly from July to October in 1955. Its cult status is based on the fact that it inspired the name of a popular rock band, Commander Cody and the Lost Planet Airmen.

"Rod Brown" ran from April 1953 to May 1954. It was set in the twenty-second century, with Rod and his Ranger companions galloping around space in their rocket ship, the *Beta,* defending the solar system against (what else?) interplanetary evil. Also starring, were: Jack Weston as Ranger Wormsey Wormser, Bruce Hall as Ranger Frank Boyle, and John Boruff as Commander Swift.

"MEN INTO SPACE" represents the beginning of an era, and a change in the public's—or at least the TV establishment's—perception of space adventure. With the launching of Russia's Sputnik in 1957 and America's Explorer in 1958, space exploration was elevated from wild fantasy to imminent reality. So in 1959, the memory of Tom Corbett of the United Solar System was put to rest and Col. Edward McCauley (William Lundigan) of the US Air Force was born.

"Men into Space" was filmed in the style of a documentary; there were no lobster men from Neptune, no Martian bank robbers. McCauley's adventures focused on problems American scientists believed a human being might actually face in space. The show was effective propaganda for the US space program, heartily supported by the Army, Navy, and Air Force.

As realistic as "Men into Space" seemed, however, few fans could have imagined they'd be watching the real thing—starring astronaut Alan Shepard—less than two years after the final episode aired.

CLASSIC LINES

SPOCK: "Highly illogical, Captain."
KIRK: "Beam us up, Scotty."
SCOTTY: "I'm doing the best I can, Captain."

"We're needed!"
[John Steed calls Emma Peel to action at the beginning of an episode of "The Avengers."]

As most fans know, science fiction TV has introduced a number of instantly recognizable catch phrases, many of which have become part of American culture.

Experts in the poll were asked to name *the* classic line of dialogue in science fiction TV, and they came up with a bunch. Interesting note: More lines are from "Star Trek" than from any other program—which indicates either how repetitous the show was or how clever its producers were in creating familiar characters. Or both. Anyway, here's what the critics picked, in no particular order:

"Kirk to *Enterprise*..."
The classic call from "Star Trek."

"Don't panic."
Advice from "The Hichhiker's Guide to the Galaxy."

"I'm a doctor, not a _____!" (fill in the blank)
McCoy's testy reply when confronted with an impossible task.

"It's a cookbook!"
The punch line from "Twilight Zone"'s chilling episode "To Serve Man."

"Imagine, if you will ..." *and* **"Submitted for your approval ..."**
Rod Serling's lead-ins to "The Twilight Zone."

"There's something moving out there."
And it's probably a slimy alien seaweed creature on "Voyage to the Bottom of the Sea."

"We will control the horizontal. We will control the vertical. ..."
From the "The Outer Limits' " opening.

"We're from France."
The Coneheads' cover story on "Saturday Night Live."

"Warning, Will Robinson, warning! Danger! Danger!"
The Robot to Will in "Lost in Space."

"Na-noo, Na-noo."
Mork's greeting on "Mork and Mindy."

"No problem!"
ALF "reassures" his sitcom family.

"The engines can't take much more of this."
Another of Scotty's warnings to Captain Kirk.

"He's dead, Jim."
"Bones" McCoy's prognosis.

"Jeepers, Mr. Kent!"
The closest Jimmy Olsen ever got to a real expletive in "Superman."

"By your command, Imperious Leader."
From "Battlestar Galactica." A gaffe. Actually, imperious *means arrogant, snotty, or overbearing. They probably meant* Imperial, *but tried to avoid copying* Star Wars *exactly.*

"Room for one more, honey."
The punch line in the "Twilight Zone" episode "Twenty-two."

"We need more power!"
Kirk pushes Scotty to get the lead out in Star Trek."

"Be seeing you."
The standard farewell in "The Prisoner."

"Have no fear, Smith is here."

RECOMMENDED READING

Volumes dealing specifically with science fiction shows:

STARLOG MAGAZINE:
Back issues contain useful information on practically every science fiction TV show ever produced. Information:
475 Park Avenue South
New York, N.Y. 10016

STAR TREK
The Making of Star Trek. Stephen Whitfield and Gene Roddenberry (Ballantine Books).

The Star Trek Compendium. Allen Asherman (Wallaby Books).

The Trouble With Tribbles. David Gerrold (Ballantine Books).

The World of Star Trek. David Gerrold (Ballantine Books).

TWILIGHT ZONE
The Twilight Zone: The Official Companion. Marc Scott Zicree (Bantam Books).

THE OUTER LIMITS
The Outer Limits: The Official Companion. David Schow and Jeffrey Frentzen (Ace Science Fiction Books).

THE HITCHHIKER'S GUIDE
The Hitchhiker's Guide to the Galaxy: The Radio Scripts. Douglas Adams (Harmony Books).

DR. WHO
Dr. Who: The Unfolding Text. John Tulloch and Manuel Alvarado (St. Martin's Press).

THE PRISONER
The Prisoner of Portmeirion. Max Hora (Number Six Publications—available through the fan club. Address on page 144).

SUPERMAN
Superman—From Serial to Cereal. Gary H. Grossman (New American Library).

BUCK ROGERS
The Collected Works of Buck Rogers in the 25th Century [Comic Strips] (Chelsea House).

BLAKE'S 7
Blake's 7: The Programme Guide. Tony Attwood (Target Books).

SUPERMARIONATION
The Anderson Files (and 75 other *Files* magazines about other shows). John Peel (New Media Publications).

ROBOTECH
The Art of Robotech. Kay Reynolds and Ardith Carlton (Donning).

GENERAL SF TV
Fantastic Television. Gary Gerani (Harmony Books). Thirteen in-depth shows., from "The Invaders" to "One Step Beyond." Additional listings.

Cult TV. John Javna (St. Martin's Press). Informal viewer's guide to 45 shows, including "The Prisoner," "Lost In Space,"etc.

Saturday Morning TV. Gary H. Grossman (Dell Books). Good section on Golden Age sf, plus cartoons and other genres.

Total Television. Alex McNeil (Penguin Books). Definitive listing of every show that's been on the air.

Complete Directory to Prime Time Network TV Shows. Tim Brooks and Earle Marsh. Definitive listing, limited to prime time shows.

The Complete Encyclopedia of Television Programs, 1947-1985. Vincent Terrace (A.S. Barnes). Definitive listing, including the most obscure shows.

The Great Television Heroes. Donald F. Glut and Jim Harmon Citadel Press. Great section on "Captain Video," "Tom Corbett," "Space Patrol," etc.

Watching TV. Walter Podrazik and Harry Castleman (McGraw Hill). Well-written history of TV, including sf shows.

GENERAL TV MAGAZINES
You never know what sf you'll find in these publications, but they're always interesting, and they're all TV.

TV Collector. P.O. Box 188, Needham, MA 02192.

RERUNS, The Magazine of Television History. P.O. Box 1057, Safford, AZ 85548

COLLECTIBLES & PHOTOS

The following list includes stores and mail order houses I've worked with at one time or another. I've always found them reputable and well-stocked, but of course this list is only for your reference—I can't guarantee them. If you write for information, be sure to send a self-addressed, stamped envelope with the letter.

The Science Fiction and Horror Emporium, Inc.
c/o Joel Eisner
Suite 129, 1671 East 16th St.,
Brooklyn, NY 11234.
(photos, models, and more)

The Cinema Shop.
604 Geary St.
San Francisco, CA 94102
(photos, videotapes of early sf TV—e.g., "Captain Video," "Captain Z-Ro")

Dudley DoRight Emporium
8218 Sunset Blvd.
Hollywood, CA 90046
(Rocky & Bullwinkle items, etc.)

Jerry Ohlinger's Movie Material Store
242 West 14th St.
New York, NY 10011
(photos)

Comic Relief
2138 University Ave.
Berkeley, CA 94704
(new and old comic books)

Larry Edmunds Book Store
6658 Hollywood Blvd.
Hollywood, CA 90028
(photos, books)

Still Things
13622 Henny Ave.
Sylmar, CA 91342
(photos, scripts, collectibles)

Hollywood Movie Posters
6727 5/8 Hollywood Blvd.
Hollywood, CA 90028
(photos)

Forbidden Planet
821 Broadway
N.Y., NY 10003
(photos, games, comics, toys, books, and more)

Chic-A-Boom
6905 Melrose
Hollywood, CA
(collectibles)

Artie Rickun
7153 W. Burleigh St.
Milwaukee, WI 53210
(collectibles)

Scooby's Toys and Collectibles
2750 Adeline St.
Berkeley, CA 94703
(collectibles)

Comics and Comix
2461 Telegraph Ave
Berkeley, CA 94704
(new and old comic books)

SOURCES

FAN CLUBS

Here are a few of the many science fiction TV fan groups in America. These are primarily organizations with which I've had personal contact, but I welcome information about others for future editions of this volume. Once again, these addresses are provided strictly for your information, without any guarantees or endorsements from the author. Be sure to send a S.A.S.E. with requests for information.

Irwin Allen Fan Club
("Voyage to the Bottom of the Sea", "Time Tunnel," "Lost In Space," "Land of the Giants")
1671 East 16th St. #129
Brooklyn, NY 11234

Dr. Who Fan Club of America
PO Box 6024
Denver, CO 80206

Companions of Dr. Who
PO Box 56764
New Orleans, LA

Blake's 7 Information Network
1305 Maywood Rd.
Richmond, VA 23229

Lost In Space Fannish Alliance
7331 Terri Robyn
St. Louis, MO 63129

Galactic Hitchhiker's Guild
("Hitchhiker's Guide")
3039 NE 181 St.
Portland, OR 97230

Barbara Bain/Martin Landau Fan Club
("Space: 1999")
c/o Terry Bowers
603 N. Clark St.
River Falls, WI

Six of One
("The Prisoner")
2426 Line Lexington Rd.
Hatfield, PA 19440

Battlestar One
PO Box 988, Astor Station
Boston, MA 02123

Star Trek Welcommittee
(publishes a guide to all "Star Trek" organizations)
PO Box 12
Saranac, MI 48881

Romance on the Rails
("Wild, Wild West")
5233 Elkhorn
Greenwell Springs, LA 70739

Scorpio
("Blake's 7")
PO Box 397
Midlothian, IL 60445